Being at Home in the World

Being at Home in the World

A New Christian Apologetic

MARK MCLEOD-HARRISON
AND
PHILIP SMITH

WIPF & STOCK · Eugene, Oregon

BEING AT HOME IN THE WORLD
A New Christian Apologetic

Wipf & Stock
An Imprint of Wipf and Stock Publishers
199 W. 8th Ave., Suite 3
Eugene, OR 97401
www.wipfandstock.com

ISBN 13: 978-1-61097-071-6

Manufactured in the U.S.A.

Dedicated to all our students,
past, present, and future.

Contents

Foreword ix
Preface xi

1   On Being Us: Who Are We, and What is This Book About? 1

2   On Being You: The Audience Who Will Read This Book 17

3   Mystery and Naturalism: Entertaining Doubts
        About Modern Naturalism 41

4   How to Think About Religion 62

5   How the Religions Address Mystery 78

6   Finding Our Place in Christ: Why We Are Christians 97

7   How to Flourish: Vocation and an Integrated Life 117

Addendum: Christian Apologetics Resources 131
Bibliography 133
Subject/Name Index 135
Scripture Index 137

Foreword

ONCE UPON A TIME, the authors attended a Society of Christian Philosophers conference with a theme of Apologetics. We were happy to attend the conference and we are long-time happy members of the Society of Christian Philosophers. We have benefited greatly from the excellent philosophical work and the warm faith of SCP members. Nevertheless, we went away disappointed from the aforementioned SCP conference. We were unhappy with what we heard. Not, of course, because of the quality of the papers or ideas presented but rather it seemed to us that the papers read at this conference were overly rationalistic, technical, and perhaps even combative. It seemed as if our philosophical compatriots thought that argument could compel fair-minded people to believe.

Now we suppose that if we asked many of those present at the conference about the role of argument in religious conversion and commitment, we would find a variety of answers and not all of them would have suggested that a person can be compelled to belief by "reason alone." But it was the tone of the conference that bothered us. But then the question arose: If a rationalistic, technical and sometime combative approach to philosophical defense and offense is not the way to argue for the faith, how should it be done? And, of course, that question is not quite right. We wanted to ask: If that is not the way to do apologetics, how should *we* do it? For we are convinced that all reasoning is personal and situated; as far as we know, no impersonal, abstract minds exist. This book is the result. It is straightforwardly personal; we say who we are and we say whom we think you, our readers are. At no point do we think our arguments will compel belief. But we do invite you to faith, and apologetics by invitation seems better than apologetics by intellectual assault. So we offer this book as a way both to do apologetics and a way to think about how it is best done.

Preface

A PREFACE OFTEN EXPLAINS how a book came to be. We do some of that in the foreword and in the text, so we won't add much here. However, we do want to express our thanks to people who have encouraged the project along the way. We presented some of our ideas in a Department of Religious Studies "Intellectual Feast," and our colleagues gave us challenging feedback. We also acknowledge encouragement and stimulation from the Forum Sunday School class at Reedwood Friends Church. We thank Patrick Allen, Provost of George Fox University, for arranging funds for editing and typesetting. We thank the many students who read earlier drafts and gave us helpful feedback; in particular we thank Joseph Delaney, who transformed scratchy drawings into tidy ".jpegs." Margaret Fuller deserves many thanks for many reasons, one of which is that she handled student requests for the early versions.

All profits from the sale of *Being at Home in the World* will be donated to the undergraduate philosophy club at GFU.

On Being Us: Who Are We,
and What is This Book About?

*Synopsis: This chapter introduces the authors and ex-
plains why we have written a book of Christian apologetics. It is important that the authors introduce themselves,
because our apologetic procedure is personal. We do not
offer a cool, detached, objective argument; instead, we
extend an invitation.*

FIRST WEEKEND OF THE semester and you're buying books. Or, like
many students these days, you checked out the required reading
list ahead of time and you're looking for used versions in on-line book-
stores. You come to *Being at Home in the World*. What's it about? After
all, *where else* can a person live, other than in the world? And who are
these authors who think they can tell you something about being where
you already are?

We are Phil Smith and Mark McLeod-Harrison, philosophy professors at George Fox University. Each of us has been teaching college
students for more than twenty years, and we think we have some insight
into our students' mindsets, particularly on questions of worldview—
ideas and beliefs about reality, knowledge and value.[1] We teach a broad

1. What is a "worldview"? A worldview is a person's general approach to living in
the world. Sometimes worldviews are carefully considered philosophies, but for some
people they consist of rough and ready ideas. A person's worldview almost always
contains answers to the main questions of philosophy: What is real? How do I know?
What is valuable? Every person has a worldview, almost always learned from the people
around him or her.

range of students, not just those majoring in philosophy. GFU requires all its students to take a class called Christian Foundations, so students from every discipline take the course. Experience teaching Christian Foundations—we both teach multiple sections most years—has led us to prepare this little book.

We fondly hope *Being at Home in the World* will be useful not just to Christian Foundations students or college students generally, but to a wide population of readers. So if you're not one of the students envisioned in the first paragraph, we welcome you too.

Loosely speaking, this is a book of "apologetics." In philosophy and theology, apologetics is the discipline of giving rational arguments for Christian beliefs. The field is called apologetics because it gives arguments in *defense* of Christianity. In a similar way, Plato's *Apology* is really the account of Socrates's defense presented to an Athenian court.

Apologetics has a long and honorable history, including such Christian thinkers as Justin Martyr in the second century, Anselm of Canterbury in the eleventh century, and C.S. Lewis, Dorothy Sayers, and Marilyn McCord Adams in the twentieth century. But this book differs significantly from the work of many contemporary Christian apologists, which is why we say it is apologetics "loosely speaking."

With a little effort on the internet, students can find dozens of websites and scores of books devoted to a rational defense of Christianity. As with just about everything on the Internet, the intellectual quality of these websites and books varies greatly. This book will probably provoke interest in some of these authors; we hope you will read carefully and critically. If you do, you will discover some really fine resources. We provide some recommendations in our appendix.

This book differs from most contemporary apologetics because we do not aim to give a rationally compelling argument for the truth of Christian doctrine. You may have heard the phrase, "a knock-down argument." We don't want to knock anybody down, literally or figuratively. We want to open a door and extend an invitation.

We want to be clear: We think there are, in fact, very good arguments for the truth of Christian beliefs. Yet to many people, these arguments are not very persuasive. Notice the difference: A good argument is not necessarily a persuasive argument. A *good* argument is one that is logically acceptable (either deductively valid or inductively strong) and based on acceptable premises (believed to be true for good reasons). In logic courses, students learn to distinguish good arguments from bad ones. A *persuasive* argument is an argument that persuades at least one person to believe something or change his mind. Obviously, some arguments persuade people without being good arguments. (Think how effective advertisements are.)

Lots of writers would lecture you at this point. You really ought to be persuaded only by good arguments, they would say. The subject matter of the argument doesn't matter. Whether it's about buying cars, believing in extraterrestrials, or voting for measure M, you should discipline yourself to be rational. Be like Mr. Spock in *Star Trek*.

Many Christian apologists argue on those lines; they try to give tight rationalistic arguments for the truth of Christian beliefs. We don't think the rationalistic arguments offered by contemporary apologists— and here we mean the good ones—are very persuasive to the kinds of students we encounter in our classrooms. As we go along, we will explain why such arguments fail to persuade people.

We observe students who apparently understand certain arguments, valid arguments using good evidence—who go away from class and simply disbelieve the conclusions of those arguments. This is true not only about arguments pertaining to religion; students are able to discount or ignore well-supported conclusions in other fields as well. Or they "believe" the conclusion of the argument on one level but completely disregard that belief when it comes to their behavior.

Please do not misinterpret what we just said. We do not think our students are stupid or particularly wicked. We think that our description of our students' thinking is also true about many people in our society. Such people seem to live "compartmentalized" lives. It's as if our students play different roles at different times in the day; in the classroom they play the role of intellectuals who render scholarly judgments, while at the mall they play the role of consumers who delight in buying whatever the advertisers tell them to desire, and at their computer consoles they play fantasy roles of many kinds. From what we observe, for many students these various roles simply exist side-by-side—jumbled, confused, and unintegrated. We will talk more about this in chapter 2 and also in chapter 7. You don't have to take our word as gospel; we ask you, the reader, to check our observations against your own experiences.

If our observations are accurate, Christian apologetics needs something more than good evidence and crystal clear reasoning. Apologetics needs to help students (and others) make connections between the various parts of their lives. Perhaps at a more basic level, it needs to infect people with a *desire* for integrated, whole lives. We worry that many individuals are apparently untroubled by intellectual and moral contradictions in their lives. In such cases apologetics needs to awaken readers' imaginations so that they might begin to dream of something better.

The "something better" to which we invite you is what we call "being at home in the world." Maybe you wonder why Christian professors would use such a phrase. Aren't Christians supposed to think of this world as temporary? An old song says: "This world is not my home; I'm just a-passing through." Why should Christians want to be at home in the world? As a first answer: When God created the world, God said that it was good. Therefore, we live in a good world. We'll say more about being at home in the world as we go along.

Before we talk further, in chapter 2, about what we see in our students, we need to say more about ourselves. If we're going to invite students to consider far-reaching and deeply personal aspects of their lives, it is only fair that we reveal something of our inner selves. But it's more than that. We object, *philosophically*, to a certain understanding of the human person, a very influential conception of what it means to be a good thinker. The view we reject is pretty familiar to most people; it is the image of the "pure thinker," the intellect who has somehow walled off her thinking self from all "distractions," such as bodily needs, emotions, and social connections. We object to the image of the purely rational, completely objective, isolated, disinterested mind. Even though famous philosophers such as Plato and Descartes praised such a mind, we do not. None of us really thinks that way, and we deceive ourselves if we think we do. God did not create us to think that way; we disapprove of the "pure thinker" even as an ideal.

Notice that a "pure thinker" is *not* at home in the world. Pure thinkers are uncomfortable with their bodies. Like Socrates and his friends in *Phaedo*, they think they will be better off the sooner they can rid themselves of their bodies and become pure souls, pure minds. Like Immanuel Kant and Jean Jacques Rousseau, they imagine that pure reason is the same for every pure thinker—and, therefore, the truly rational thinker doesn't really *need* other minds. After all, other pure thinkers will only think what I think anyway, right?

We repeat our point: God did not make us to be pure thinkers. When human beings believe and know, they do so as embodied people with emotions and social relationships. Therefore, since in this book we are going to talk about some of our most important beliefs, we have to explain a little about our history.

PHIL SMITH

I was raised in a devout Christian family. We attended church services at East Wenatchee Friends Church on Sunday morning and evening and prayer meeting on Wednesday evening. We lived about forty minutes' driving time away from the church, but the distance did not deter my parents. Even when my father's factory shift required him to work Sunday mornings he drove the family to Wenatchee at four o'clock in the morning to drop us at my older sister's house. That way she could take the rest of us to church, and Dad would pick us up after working his shift.

The name tells you our church was a Quaker church. It doesn't tell you that this particular church, like many other Friends churches in the western United States, had been influenced by the holiness movement. "Holiness" names a theological movement among some Protestant churches, such as Nazarenes, Free Methodists, Wesleyans, and the Salvation Army. These are relatively new denominations, forming in the nineteenth and twentieth centuries. Holiness churches emphasize the work of the Holy Spirit in Christians' lives. Of course, all orthodox (Trinitarian) Christian churches affirm belief in the Holy Spirit. But preachers in the holiness movement proclaimed a bold message of personal transformation by means of the Spirit's work—think of Salvation Army "officers" (really, ordinary members of the church) working with poor people in London's slums in the 1890s, or Nazarene preachers proclaiming freedom from sin (including alcoholism) in the cities and towns of the western U.S. in the 1930s. Now, the Salvation Army and the Nazarene church are not terribly large, so maybe you're not familiar with these examples. The point is that the holiness movement preached that the Holy Spirit would make a dramatic difference in the way believers live.

Sadly, sometimes the holiness movement slipped into legalism. The mark of the Spirit's work in a person's life became conformity to a list of rules: no movies, no alcohol, no tobacco, no gambling, etc. As a young person growing up in a church marked by this tradition, I imbibed some of its legalistic attitudes. For instance, as a trombone player in high school, I was invited to play in a jazz band (a permitted activity), but I felt great reluctance when the band was invited to play for an Elks Club dance (dancing was not okay, so how could I play for a dance?). At the same time, I had a sense that there was something deeper and truer in holiness theology, something better than legalistic rule-keeping. Decades later, I still appreciate the spiritual sensitivity of the holiness movement and its enthusiasm for personal transformation, even though I think many of its rules were wrong-headed.

I enrolled at George Fox College in 1973. Here I learned more about Quaker beliefs and practices. Quaker ideas had not been denied at East Wenatchee Friends, but they hadn't been emphasized either. I learned that prayer includes listening to God, rather than only asking or thanking God. I learned that the Bible supports equality between men and women, both in family life and in the church (even though many Bible-loving Christians deny this). I learned that Christians ought to be peacemakers—and they actually can be peacemakers, not just reluctant warriors. And I learned that Christians should care about social justice issues, especially overcoming racism.

There is a link between the holiness theology of my youth and the Quaker beliefs of my adulthood. Both movements emphasize that believers can experience God *now*. Religion ought to be experiential; it ought to connect to real life. It should not be a matter of beliefs alone, nor yet beliefs plus a rigorous set of moral expectations. Both movements say that God's work in our lives is gracious and loving.

College also exposed me to the almost overwhelming challenges to Christian faith of the modern era. I studied at a Christian college where professors and friends were eager to support my faith, so I suppose other young Christians who went to state universities or explicitly secular colleges might have faced harder challenges. Maybe. Or maybe the difference lies mostly in the student and not so much in the school. In any case, my struggles with belief in God began in college and continued for many years afterward.

In my experience, religious doubt created anxiety and unhappiness. At many times I was aware that I *wanted* to believe in God, and I worried that my desire to believe in God might lead me astray. Maybe my belief in God was only a matter of *wish fulfillment*. My worry was a classic example of a modern challenge to faith.

In philosophy, we date the modern period from René Descartes, who lived from 1596–1650.[2] So when I speak of the "almost overwhelming challenges of the modern era," I am talking about a long period of time and a *great many* ideas that have come together to produce challenges to Christian faith. The idea that troubled me so much in my college years is an example of a general category of problems, a category I will call "suspicion."

There are different versions of suspicion. Karl Marx said that people often believe things because those beliefs support their economic interests. Friedrich Nietzsche said people often believe things as an expression of their will to power. Sigmund Freud said that people often believe things in order to repress unacceptable desires. Do you see the point? Each of these influential thinkers said, in effect: "People hold certain beliefs, and they think they have good reasons for these beliefs, but in reality their beliefs are caused by something else (by their economic self-interest, by desire for self-assertion, or by unconscious drives and wishes)."

These apostles of suspicion did not give good arguments for their conclusions. They hardly gave arguments at all. Instead, they merely asserted their position. Nevertheless, the suspicions they planted were very effective. Many people in the twentieth century found themselves pulled away from their political, aesthetic, moral, or religious beliefs because of Marx, Nietzsche, or Freud.

Each brand of suspicion has impacted many people in our society in the last hundred years. I think the Freudian version bothered me most when I was in college. How can I believe in God when I want to believe in God? How can I be sure that I am not just deceiving myself? Is it possible that my "religious experiences" are really nothing more than projections of my desires?

We will say more about suspicion in chapter 3, but we will turn suspicion against a different target. But for now, it is enough to see

2. Many late twentieth century philosophers claimed that the modern era ended sometime in the twentieth century. Most college students are familiar with the claim that we live in a "postmodern" age. In lectures, I've often used 1650–1950 as a convenient time frame for the modern period. But I think it's too early to be sure of such historical judgments. The women and men who write the history of philosophy texts in coming centuries will be able to make a better call.

that in the nineteenth and twentieth centuries, Marx, Nietzsche, and Freud—each with his own doctrine—undermined many people's beliefs about politics, social relationships, religion, art, and many other things. Gradually the outlines of a modern worldview emerged, a worldview that is widely assumed to be true, though it is not often explicitly stated. The main feature of the modern worldview is that it is *closed to mystery*. The philosopher Gabriel Marcel has pointed out that the modern worldview has lots of room for problems, but no room for mystery. Problems are questions to which we don't have the answer—yet. How much food can we grow without polluting the environment? What is the optimum tax rate if the goal is maximizing tax revenue? How many craters are there on the moon? But *mystery* has to do with deeper questions. Mystery touches something fundamental to the human person. Why are some things so beautiful that they make you cry? How is it possible that some people torture and murder other people? What can we hope for in life? Why are we here?

In chapter 3 we will turn suspicion against the modern worldview. We will invite our readers to *open* themselves to mystery. We will give arguments to back up our invitation—after all, we're philosophers and that's what philosophers do. But if we really are in a postmodern age, we expect the invitation will be more persuasive than the arguments.

Back to my story. After college I still believed in God, though my beliefs coexisted with painful doubts. It took me many years to realize that *doubts are part of faith*. I can live a faithful life, I can grow in my love for God, and I can recognize the grace of God in my life *and still experience periods of doubt*. God intends for us to become mature spiritual beings, so he doesn't always give us feelings of certainty and light. He "withdraws" for a while (only in the sense that we don't feel him; in reality, God is everywhere always) so we can walk "on our own," so to speak. I have continued to believe in God, and I have made many important life decisions based on my belief in God, but I still have doubts.

I attended Fuller Seminary, and I served as pastor for two Friends churches in the 1980s. Then I did graduate work at the University of Oregon, finishing my PhD in Philosophy in 1991. I began teaching part-time at George Fox in 1982, and I've been full-time since 1992. So most of my career has centered on teaching. Along the way, I have written some philosophy books and lots of conference papers and articles. I wrote a fantasy-adventure novel called *The Heart of the Sea*, and I'm working on a murder mystery story. But I still love teaching most of all. I like explaining ideas to students and seeing them come alive to the implications of ideas.

I want to think my life is like a well-woven blanket. My teaching, my philosophical writings, my sermons and devotional writings, my novels, and other things I haven't talked about here (family life, local politics, etc.) are all tied together by Jesus Christ. Now, if Jesus is not the Son of God, as I believe he is, then I am deeply deceived about my life. If Jesus is merely some dead guy from two thousand years ago, my life is a bundle of rags that don't match or fit together.

You can see that I am speaking very frankly now. I am revealing my heart. The topic of this book is burningly important to me. The coherence of the life I have lived depends on the things we discuss in this book. This is, I think, as it should be. Our religious beliefs are not just a matter of cool, rational debate. Our deepest fears, hopes, and passions are wrapped up in our religious beliefs.

MARK MCLEOD-HARRISON

In 1967, I was eleven years old. July 1 of that year was the one hundredth anniversary of Canada's confederation. Orillia, Ontario, my hometown, was coincidentally celebrating its first hundred years as well. Celebrations abounded—parades, shows of old farm equipment, and fairs remembering the past. The World's Fair, Expo '67, was held in Montreal. My whole family, including my grandparents, visited Expo '67—a rare adventure for us. Back home, I dressed for a parade in a tie, elastic armbands, and a barbershop quartet hat, clothes of a by-gone era. In such times of remembrance, many elderly people were interviewed about the old days, when horses still ruled the roads, the telephone was a novel invention, and only the very wealthy enjoyed indoor plumbing. My great grandmother was in her seventies, my grandparents in their middle fifties, and my parents in their thirties. Excluding my great-grandmother, none of the rest of us would have counted as a potential interviewee. I don't remember her being interviewed, but I suppose she was old enough. I do, however, recall the announcement of the first successful heart transplant which took place in December 1967. I remember thinking, given all the new advances in medicine, that perhaps when Canada celebrated its bicentennial in 2067 I would be one of the elderly people being interviewed about life in the old days in Orillia.

I'm not sure now that I want to live to be one hundred and eleven years old, and I haven't lived in Orillia for thirty-five years. Yet I'm more convinced than ever that with age comes the possibility of wisdom—but only the possibility. Wisdom does not, I've discovered, fall out of the sky on its own. It does, however, come to those who seek it. Looking back at the mere fifty-plus years of my life, I hope I've reached some wisdom. I know, however, that any I've reached, I've not reached alone. I also know that a good deal of any wisdom I've garnered has come through my faith in Jesus. I also know that my faith in Jesus was often, although not always, tied to questions and doubts through which I often agonized and wept.

I might say, as an aside, that there are different kinds of doubt, depending on the thing you doubt and the place of that thing in your life. I'll talk more about this in chapter 6.

Wisdom evolves in community through history. My parents, grandparents, and great-grandmother all contributed to whatever understanding of life I have. So did other larger communities, especially the various church communities in which I've attempted to live out my Christian commitments. I was raised in a Baptist church. Our family went to church every Sunday, my parents were involved in youth ministry, and my father once received a call to pastor a church, though he declined the invitation. My mother taught Sunday school and worked in the nursery for many years; she's still active there. My father died in 1993, and though my grandfather and great grandmother also passed on, my grandmother still sits in her care home, thinking of the old days. She is ninety-nine. Each of these persons was or is a Christian.

The year 1967 was important not just for Canada and Orillia, but also for my spiritual life, for that was the year I committed myself to being a follower of Jesus. My church taught that the Bible was God's word to humans and it could be trusted. Jesus, as described in the Scriptures, was alive and real and with us. I recall being given a Gideon New Testament at the public school. (Canada doesn't have the same understanding of the separation of Church and state as the United States does.) Many of my friends quickly wrote their name in the front, as did I. But at the back was a place to sign when and if you had "given your heart" to Jesus. I knew, from Sunday school, that I had not. But later that year, I knelt by my bed and committed my life to following Jesus.

That conversion experience was very important, one of many turning points for me. As a Baptist, I'd been raised to understand that becoming a Christian was something a person decided to do. I had never been told that other people were born into faith and grew into it by a sort of osmosis. My Episcopalian and Roman Catholic friends, of course, were baptized as babies. Followed up by confirmation by the bishop later, for them the process of becoming a Christian stretched out over a long period of time. For some it stuck; for others it did not. Yet the same is true for many Baptists. Going forward at an altar call or praying the "sinner's prayer" does not always mean that someone takes on the Christian life and all its commitments. But my 1967 prayer did stick. Of course, I had my times when I doubted. In fact, many times. I would describe a good deal of my life into my thirties as the life of a skeptical believer. Modernism had done its work well. Sometimes, too, I deliberately and consciously went against my own Christian commitments. Yet overall, I couldn't get away from the deep sense—a personal sort of quiet, experiential knowledge—that if I was going to live my life well, I would have to confront my questions about Jesus and ultimately live my life in relation to Jesus himself. So I began my long, stretched-out journey toward Jesus by questioning his reality.

As a teenager, during what was often called the "Jesus People" or "Jesus Freak" movement, several of us formed a Bible-study and evangelism group under the influence of Campus Crusade for Christ's "Explo'72." Explo '72 was a massive youth rally held in Dallas, Texas to which a number of my friends traveled to hear Johnny Cash and Kris Kristofferson perform and Billy Graham preach. That small gathering of teenagers grew over the next year to be a regular weekly meeting of about fifty to seventy youth from many different churches in our area. We had monthly outreaches featuring Christian rock bands; these grew, at their peak, to around three hundred people. Our oldest member, who became our leader, was in his early twenties. Those were exciting times for the young Christians of Orillia and deeply formative in my spiritual growth. I came to know not only Baptist but also Presbyterian, Episcopal, Pentecostal, Assemblies of God, Brethren, Mennonite, and Roman Catholic Christians. I have to admit, however, that most of us still thought of Roman Catholic Christians as needing "salvation" Baptist-style (and no doubt, they thought we needed to take the Eucharist!). What I learned, perhaps most profoundly, was that Christianity is diverse and wonderfully so. It took me many years, however, to understand how Jesus could be so differently understood while at the same time be the same Jesus.

During the summer of 1973, a young Brethren woman from our interdenominational youth group, whom I happened to be dating, began to speak in tongues at some meeting she had attended.[3] As a Baptist, I had been taught that speaking in tongues was not something available to present-day Christians. Yet I was having really deep questions about the truth of Christianity at the time. My emotional and spiritual life was all over the place, like a car on a slippery, winding mountain road. I went with her and several other friends to a Pentecostal meeting where I was urged to pray for the gift of tongues. But when I prayed to receive the gift, nothing happened. I wasn't feeling very spiritual or particularly open to God. So in a very dramatic (to me at least) and pretty arrogant manner, I marched up the central aisle, through the doors, out of the church and away from God. My friend came to speak with me later and wisely counseled that not everyone receives all the spiritual gifts. But in that moment when I left the building, I felt I had left God behind.

Before I rejected God, I had applied to a Bible college. For one reason or another, admission to the college was delayed. Several weeks after leaving God behind, the letter of acceptance arrived. It dawned on me that if I was serious about knowing the truth about God (if only to more knowledgably reject God), I had better know something about the Bible. So, later that summer I packed up and left home for what was then a quite strict Bible college. Long hair for men was not permitted, dating was very limited and monitored quite closely, lights went out by eleven o'clock at night, and every student was expected at breakfast as well as daily chapel. My parents worried about such strictness, but the discipline was good for me. I took to it like a salmon to a Northwest river. Yet I had arrived on the steps of a Bible college not really believing the Bible and certainly not trusting God! Nevertheless, I learned a good deal of Bible content, and after a few weeks, I became convinced that my feelings of faith might come and go but the Faith did not. Jesus was still the same, even if I wasn't. So I grew spiritually by reading Scripture and being involved in a great deal of Christian service—everything from hospi-

---

3. Some Christian groups teach that at some point in believers' lives the Holy Spirit will "fill" them. The mark of the Holy Spirit's filling people is "speaking in tongues." Believers speak words to God or to other people in languages unknown to them.

tal and elder-care visitation to teaching Sunday school, preaching, and mission work overseas. Although there were moments when I confused the more or less rote discipline of the school with spiritual discipline, I still managed to fall in love with the Bible—but more importantly, with Jesus. It was at Bible college that I first learned about the development of the canon of Scripture and some of the challenges of Biblical studies. But it was also there that I first encountered a philosophy class. My faith took a decidedly intellectual turn. I wanted so much to be able to prove that Christianity was true. I was fired up by apologetics—the defense of the faith—and wanted to show everyone how true Christianity was. I now think that I wanted to prove it to myself. Even though Jesus wasn't leaving me, I still was fundamentally a skeptical believer.

Philosophy, I thought, held the keys to dealing with my doubt. After Bible college, I headed off to a Christian liberal arts college in the United States (never, as it turned out, to live in Canada again except for a few weeks at a stretch). There I took up philosophy with a vengeance. I earned a BA in philosophy, then an MA in philosophy of religion from an evangelical seminary, and finally an MA and a PhD in philosophy from a secular university in California. I fell in love with philosophy but understanding Christianity and showing it was true were never far from my mind. By the end of my doctoral studies, however, I had shifted from trying to show that Christianity was true to attempting to show how it could be rational to be a Christian, a more modest and reachable goal.

While in my doctoral studies and then later when I taught at the evangelical Christian college up the street, I attended an Evangelical Covenant church pastored by a very thoughtful friend from whom I learned a great deal. His commitment as a Christian was deep, and it showed in his wisdom in dealing with various church challenges and the guidance he gave in my life. I was also part of a men's Bible study—early morning, every Wednesday before work—with a diverse set of members. There was an architect, a retired English professor, a computer wizard, a biology professor, some business professionals, a truck driver, a librarian, and others. The various insights from these friends helped me to see God at work in a variety of ways of living out one's faith in Jesus.

Then my family and I moved to Texas, which, for me, was like the Israelites' desert wandering. My (late) wife became very ill during our time there (later, she died of complications of the illness), and we couldn't find a church where we felt at home. Still a Christian, I was driven more and more into skepticism at the evils in my life and the deep loneliness we felt in our time there. But one of my students invited us to attend a healing service at an Episcopal church—St. Andrew's. I went, but reluctantly, since I had long before rejected the "splashier" spiritual gifts such as divine healing and tongues-speaking—remember my arrogant response to not receiving the gift of speaking in tongues? Yet something marvelous happened at that first healing service. As the priest prayed for us, I sensed in a very powerful way that Jesus was in—no, that Jesus was—the priest. We went back week after week, found a place where the spiritual gifts were alive and well and, in a good Episcopalian manner, orderly. It was a great time of healing for me spiritually, and it eventually led to my sense of call into the priesthood. I found the daily prayer book readings and prayers immensely rich and helpful, and various sorts of meditational practices nurtured my soul. I began to read all sorts of literature on mysticism, spiritual disciplines, and prayer. It was all thoroughly Christian even though far from my Baptist roots. I discovered, again, the diversity of ways in which Jesus is real.

After a few years, I received a job offer at George Fox University where I currently teach. During my time there, I met my wife Susan. She, too, has been a deep influence on my spiritual growth. In particular, she has helped me see more clearly that my social interactions with people are not always generous, that various sorts of anger from my childhood and former painful experiences need not continue, and that the Gospel is as much about helping the poor and doing social justice as it is about heavenly salvation. I've come to see more truly that marriage is a sacrament, a means through which the grace of God can be made more present.

There are literally dozens of other important events and people who do not show up in this short version of my spiritual life. Yet I hope this gives a lively sense of the importance of people and the pursuit of Jesus in my life. The important thing, though, is not my life but the fact that *Jesus is rooted in history and in various communities.* In my case, those communities are primarily Baptist, Evangelical Covenant, and Episcopalian. But I've learned too from Quakers, Mennonites, Charismatics, and Roman Catholics, among others. The amazing thing is that Jesus is alive and well in all these communities. Jesus is the Rabbi, the King of Kings, the Cosmic Christ, the Son of Man, Christ Crucified, the Monk who Rules the World, the Bridegroom of the Soul, the True Image, the Liberator, and the Good, the True, and the Beautiful.[4] Yet Jesus is the same yester-

---

4. See Pelikan, *Jesus through the Centuries* for a wonderful study of various ways

day, today, and forever. The Jesus who lived, died, and was resurrected two thousand years ago is alive and well and living in my household, in my community, as he is alive and well and living in many millions of other households and thousands of other communities.

My experience of Jesus has always been embedded in a community, whether the small community of my family, the larger community of a local church, or the even larger community of a particular denomination. My love of Jesus has been through a great deal of doubting and a generous amount of evil and suffering. Yet Jesus has never left me, even when I often times wanted to leave him. I see him in Susan and in my sons, Ian and Micah. I see him in my colleagues at George Fox, and in any number of people in the Church. I see Jesus in the poor, in those against whom injustice is done, and in those who have stood against those injustices. I see Jesus in the beauty of little bean sprouts poking their heads through my sandy garden soil, in the small wild-flower garden Susan planted, and in the beauty of a well-written novel or a pot thrown by my potter friend. My Jesus is alive on the pages of Scripture but also in the prayer book, the love of my little boy for vacuum cleaners, and the thoughts of my hometown where I first knew love. And Jesus, I trust, is alive in me.

PREVIEW: THE REST OF THIS BOOK

In this book we *invite* our readers to recognize the deep *mystery* of human life, a mystery that we will never fully understand. We think that God, as revealed in Jesus, is the center of mystery. God has created human beings in such a way that we find our true selves as we journey deeper and deeper into God's love. True human happiness—what philosophers call *"flourishing"*—comes into human lives that are integrated by *God's call.*

The italicized words in the last paragraph indicate the main themes of our book: invitation, mystery, flourishing, and God's call. We are not going to give forceful arguments that compel anyone to do anything. We are not going to answer every question. But we are going to invite you to something wonderful.

Here's an outline of the book. First, in chapter 2, we will talk a little about you; in particular, we'll describe philosophical currents that probably have influenced you. We'll recount some history of philoso-

---

Jesus has been understood.

phy in order to explain our current modern/postmodern situation. In chapter 3, we begin our "apology" for Christian faith by examining and criticizing modern naturalism, a prominent worldview that excludes all religious belief. We do not intend to refute modern naturalism, but we do offer strong reasons to doubt its truth. If modern naturalism is not satisfying, people are free to re-examine religion. Before we discuss the world's religions, in chapter 4 we talk about how to think about religion in general. In chapter 5, we explain why we prefer Christianity to the other great religions, even though we find very good features in each of them. (For instance, they are all preferable to modern naturalism.) Chapter 6 turns personal; each author explains why he is a Christian. Given our overall philosophical position (that human beings are created to be at home in the world), it follows that our reasons for faith must be personal. Finally, in chapter 7, we explain the idea of an integrated life, and we invite readers to join us in finding integration in the community of faith.

2

On Being You: The Audience
Who Will Read This Book

*Synopsis: In this chapter we describe postmodern readers.
First, we invite you to see yourself in a classroom fable.
You needn't be a student to connect with the scene. Then
we explain what we mean by "postmodern" by telling a
bit of philosophical history.*

IMAGINE YOURSELF SITTING IN a classroom with a teacher talking about the science of porcine production of insulin. You are taking a biology course for non-majors, a general education course you are required to take but in which your interest easily lags. You've never heard the term "porcine" before and your laptop is open in front of you, so you look up the word. But since the internet is now open and the world is at your fingertips, you start surfing around and find out about a book discussing porcine philosophy and religion. That seems intriguing, so you cruise around some more and discover a funny website where the author lampoons the publishers of the book for not allowing some pictures from the original book to be shown on the web, even though the book is out of print. You start to wonder about intellectual property rights, since you have an ethics class assignment on the same subject, so you think you'll look that up, but not before you have to suppress a laugh over the funny pictures on the website. So you text your friend across the room, and she looks up the site that caused your chuckle. Now she's smiling and her friend is looking over her shoulder and smiling too. Meanwhile, you've gone on to intellectual property rights and found this great rave about why it's okay to download copyrighted music to your iPod without paying. Of course, you or at least some of your friends have been doing this since you were old enough to push the right buttons on your computer. You've listened to such music repeatedly. You start writing down some thoughts you have when the teacher calls you by name and asks about the importance of porcine insulin for the diabetic human. Of course, you have no idea, since you didn't do the reading for today's class, having spent a good deal of last night at a really interesting Bible study that happened to cover the passage in James about the power and potential evil of the human tongue. Before you do anything else, the idea pops into your mind that your ideas are yours and need not be accessed by this teacher who has just asked you the question. What is the source of this thought? Your emotions, your reason, or both?

Of course, this question shouldn't distract you, since your teacher awaits a reply. At this point, you can do one of several things. You can guess, since you vaguely remember your great uncle talking about the old days when, he said, the insulin he took made him more pork-like—cuddly and pink. But you are not sure. Or you can lie, and tell your teacher you aren't feeling good and get up to leave. Or you can tell the truth, which is that you don't have a clue what the answer is, having been otherwise occupied both during class and last night, although you have some interesting information about intellectual property rights at your fingertips.

So ends our imaginary trip through your biology class.

FLOURISHING

You might be wondering what porcine insulin, intellectual property rights, philosophy, religion, the Bible, and truth-telling all have to do with each other. Nevertheless, we suggest that, in fact, these things may be more intimately connected than a first glance might indicate. We can summarize the connection in one word: flourishing.

"Flourishing" is the word contemporary philosophers use to refer to what ancient and medieval philosophers would have called "the good life." Contemporary philosophers avoid "the good life" for two reasons. First, in popular culture, the good life is often associated with a life of ease, material plenty, and pleasure; historically, no philosophical school (not even the Epicureans) taught that the good life consisted of such things. Second, and more importantly, contemporary philosophers want to distance themselves from the particular visions of the good life endorsed by various ancient and medieval philosophers. According to

Aristotle, a truly good life is only available to men of a certain social class who develop intellectual and moral virtues. According to Thomas Aquinas, the truly good life is lived in accordance with natural law and aims at eternal happiness in God's presence. And so on—many ancient and medieval philosophers described various visions of the good life. Contemporary philosophers object to many aspects of these traditional ideas; for example, they reject Aristotle's sexist belief that women are by nature irrational beings who cannot achieve truly good lives.

By adopting the term "flourishing," philosophers today can talk about the basic idea of the good life without buying into controversial concepts, such as the idea that there is a purpose or goal for human life, or the idea that people should be rightly related to God. In the end, we think human flourishing *does* involve living for a purpose and being rightly related to God, but for now we are using the word as other philosophers do.

We want to connect human flourishing with the notion of personal integration and wisdom. People have long thought being integrated as a human person is important. At a minimum, integration means the different parts of one's life all fit together. The ancient Greek thinkers thought and taught about the virtues, all of which were thought to be united in one virtue—the Good. In religious terms, we might say that integration rests in God. (We'll say more about integration in chapter 7.)

Living a flourishing and hence integrated life is, in one way, the main thrust of this book. The question is: how to do it. This has always been the question. Yet we think the ground has shifted beneath us culturally. It is more difficult now to see not only how to live an integrated life but also why we should. We have noticed that present day students do not seem to think the same way students of our era did, or even students of twenty years ago. In the "old days," integration, or the lack there of, seemed simply a problem of hard work. It was commonly thought that the world was itself "of a piece," that is, unified at some underlying level. There was, in fact, a Truth or a Reality (even if very mysterious!) that one could search for or appeal to in order to strive toward an integrated life. Of course, there were many disagreements over what that Truth or Reality was. Nevertheless, it was held that there was something to look for. The earliest Western philosophers appear to have thought so, along with other prominent thinkers throughout Western history. In very recent times, this all seems to have changed. Many people aren't sure there is a Reality or Truth to be found. Many do not believe in a ground of unity underneath our experiences.

There are just our experiences. Reality seems to have disappeared and what is left is whatever we make or think or feel. It is hard to see, then, why we should try to live an integrated life. There appears little connection between integration and flourishing.

Through the modern period, philosophers thought that a human being could uncover the basic framework or foundation for living a unified and whole life. Now, before we go any further, we want to clarify: For most of human history what most people thought about was making sure they had enough food to eat, a place to rest their heads, and some clothes to wear! The vast majority of people had little leisure time to think about much beyond the basic necessities. Most of what we often think of as intellectual work was done by the wealthy or the otherwise privileged. That is, at least the intellectual work that was recorded. All of the thinkers we'll talk about in this chapter were men and generally fairly privileged men at that. We do not want to disparage the millions of other people who lived—often times quite well in terms of the sorts of things we think are important to flourishing—without formal education. But since so little of what those millions thought and believed was recorded or, when it was recorded (as in the case of many women who wrote), it was ignored, we are going to talk mostly about men and their intellectual influence. We do this in full recognition of the bias it brings to our story. We're not happy about this bias, so we at least want to acknowledge it openly.

To return to our story, many philosophers thought that true reality and the source for a unified life could be found if one looked for it. One could discover it and then come to know it. Socrates, for example, felt he was called by God to spend his life searching for wisdom. Wisdom was something real, something a person could understand and conform her life to. Augustine thought something similar, although he thought knowing oneself was a mirror for knowing God. Having found God, that knowledge would shed light on how to live a whole and unified life. Although early philosophers such as Plato tended to divide humans into more or less discrete parts—reason, emotions, will—they still thought life was united, if nothing else by the ordering of its disparate parts.

One of the questions we need to answer in thinking about the integration of the human person—about flourishing—is what is the human person? In the modern period, as we indicated earlier, the human person came to be thought of as a sort of strictly thinking entity—Descartes's "thinking thing." The emphasis came to be on reason, pure reason, detached from will, emotions, desires, bodily or social condition. Of course, these other things were taken to exist, but they were less important. Once you came to understand yourself as a pure, thinking self, then the rest of one's life could be ordered around the disembodied, unemotional, de-socialized thinking thing. We said in the last chapter that we object to the image of the purely rational, completely objective, isolated, disinterested mind. As we said before, none of us really thinks that way, and we deceive ourselves if we think we can.

Today many people, the so-called "postmodern" generation—that is, your generation—don't think of the human person in the modernist way. Yet today's culture has not returned to the pre-modern beliefs about the person either. Instead, we have moved to an even more disintegrated notion of the person, or perhaps to the thought that there really are no persons at all. In the rest of this chapter we want very briefly to present the Western history of the human self and how we got, intellectually, to the place we are. We will describe how, in fact, many of us seem to function in our postmodern situation. We promise to return to the question about how porcine insulin production, philosophy, religion, and the rest are connected together. But we think it helpful, if not vital, for our readers to get at least a glimpse of how we got to postmodernity in the first place. So here we go on a history of Western philosophical thought. This is an absurdly large task for a ridiculously limited number of pages! Think of this as a historical sampler, analogous to a sampler of chocolate at See's Candy.

Timeline

```
---------Ancient Philosophy------------        -----------Medieval Philosophy----------
BCE                               CE
500               0               500              1000              1500
Socrates      Epicurus        Augustine                        Aquinas
Plato
Aristotle
```

```
                   -----------------------Modern Philosophy-----------------------------
1600        1700            1800              1900              2000
Descartes   Locke           Kant      Kierkegaard      Camus
Spinoza     Berkeley                       Nietzsche
Leibniz     Hume
```

(Notice that the scale of the timeline changes in the modern period.)

PLATO

Let's begin with Plato (we've already left out several hundred years!). Plato believed that humans (along with many other things) had an essence, that is, something that makes a thing the thing it is. So, for example, trees are what they are because they contain the essence "treeness." Humans, thus, are human by virtue of their "humanness." There is something about us—whatever it may be—that makes us human as opposed to porcine, bovine, feline, etc. (By now we hope you've looked up "porcine," if you needed to, but if you haven't, it has to do with being a pig—"bovine" has to do with being a cow.) Plato's essences existed on their own, independent of the things we see around us, in a sort of serene majesty out there, free of the physical universe. Everything you see around you, including humans, "participate" in the essences out there. Plato believed in God, but the divine was limited by the essences in what it could make or do. Plato's God had to fashion the world we see around us according to what was found among the essences. What is really important here, though, is that when humans came to be, they came to be according to the essence of the human. "Essence precedes existence"—just like a blueprint precedes a house. The human essence was found in the soul, and humans were made of a soul and a body, with the soul being the primary aspect of a human.

ARISTOTLE

Aristotle, Plato's student, also believed in essences. However, he thought essences were not "free-floating" but rather in the things themselves. Humans thus were essence/matter combinations (or "enformed matter"). One could not find a human without both. We don't just participate in the human essence. We *are* our human essence.[1] One could say that Aristotle and Plato would agree: "No essence, no existence." For both Plato and Aristotle, because of the fact that we humans share an essence—that is, at our core natures, we are the same—humans have the same structure of morality and meaning. What gives my life meaning is, at some very basic level, the same thing that gives you meaning, and the

---

1. Aristotle was not perfectly consistent in his teaching, for in some places he suggests that the reasonable part of the soul could outlive the body. If that is true, then after death souls are not enformed matter, and dead bodies are just objects, not enformed matter. However that may be, according to Aristotle, while we live on earth we surely are biological as well as soulish entities.

flourishing life (including ethical treatment of one another), is rooted in the same basic framework for all persons.

One of the important differences between the Platonic and the Aristotelian understandings of the human person, however, is the role of the emotions. While both of course believed in the emotional aspects of humans, Plato seemed less willing to let emotions have as central a role in the picture of humanity than Aristotle did. For Plato, reason should rule the emotions and our basic drives. His image is a charioteer driving two horses, where the charioteer is reason, and one horse is our spiritual (or emotional) component and the other our appetites. While Aristotle too has reason rule supreme (in the end), he at least allows for a more central role for emotions. For example, Plato suggested that poetry and the theatre are misleading and, in fact, should be censored in an ideal state. Aristotle believed that attending a tragedy could purge our emotions, providing catharsis. In the end, however, both thinkers thought of the human person as fundamentally rational, with emotions and the appetites playing a secondary role. When the various parts of a person were well ordered (reason in control of emotions and appetites), the *whole* person flourished.

We think Aristotle's emphasis on the social nature of human beings is more realistic than Plato's emphasis on the pure rational soul. Ironically, however, Aristotle's views seem to be more overtly sexist than Plato's. Aristotle thought that women were by nature less rational than men (and anyone who paid close attention to men and women could see this). Thus, women's natural roles would center on caring for children and attending to the needs of husbands; you would never expect a woman to be a philosopher or to participate in ruling the state. Plato, on the other hand, imagined that in the ideal state the ruling class would consist of purely intellectual philosophers. On his view, it was possible for the soul of a woman to achieve freedom from the concerns of the body, that is, to become a pure mind. So he left open the possibility that women could be rulers along with men.

We agree with many contemporary feminists that Plato's view—though it seems friendlier to women because it grants them a kind of equality with men—exacts a very high price. Plato makes women equal to men only when we consider men and women as pure, isolated minds. Most feminists today recognize that the "pure thinker" doesn't exist and that philosophers (men) have almost always modeled ideal pure thinkers after themselves. What we need is a view of human nature and human flourishing that recognizes the social nature of human beings *and* sees male and female as genuinely equal. Rather than explain how we think that can be done, we will return to our historical survey. We leave the question for the reader to ponder: Is there a way to understand human nature as thoroughly social (not pure thinkers) that also values women equally with men?

AUGUSTINE

About three hundred years after Aristotle, Jesus taught that God created the world, including humans. In accordance with Jewish thinking, Jesus taught that humans were made in the image of God. Three hundred years after Jesus, the message of the Christian gospel won the Western world. Christianity became the official religion of the state of Rome. About six years later, St. Augustine was converted. Augustine read his Plato, and took what he could as an explanatory framework for his work in theology and philosophy. He taught that Plato's essences had been in the mind of God forever (or perhaps created by God, but still in God's mind), and when the world was divinely created, little essential seeds (*rationes seminales*) were placed into the world. As the world unfolds, the essences of things shape the way things are. Thus, humans have an essence, just as Plato and Aristotle believed. In the context of Christianity, however, this essence is given by God. God creates the essences of things (or they exist in God's thoughts) rather than floating free "out there." What allows for human ethics and meaning is the image of God in us, something we all share in virtue of the divinely supplied essence. Again, essence precedes existence, for essences are first in the mind of God and then in nature and in us.

The Augustinian model was deeply influential in the West partly because the Platonic framework was so conducive to developing biblical thought but partly because Aristotle's works were lost for centuries. Some Muslim scholars reintroduced Aristotle to the Church, however, and in the twelfth century Thomas Aquinas used Aristotle as a framework for re-developing Christian theology. For our purposes here, the main issue is that the idea of the human essence, captured in the middle ages by the notion of the image of God, continued to influence and shape how Western humans thought of themselves. God made the world, including humans, and we are made after the divinely rooted essences.

DESCARTES

We now skip to the beginnings of the modern period, which is typically traced to Descartes, although there are earlier developments that lay out the groundwork for Descartes. Until the modern period, it was largely thought that reality is what it is and that the human essence, via reason, enabled us to grasp things about the nature of reality. How we come to know things was typically considered a secondary issue to how things are. One could first answer the question "what is real" and then answer the question "how do we know." Metaphysics (what is real) preceded epistemology (how we know). With Descartes, the order is reversed. He thought the question of how we know things should come first. Instead of just accepting reality as we think about it, we should question first whether how we think about it is correct. So he set out on his famous "method of doubt," which has three stages. (1) Have your senses ever deceived you? Then might they be deceiving you now? (2) Have you ever had a dream so vivid and real-seeming that you couldn't tell your dream-state from your awake-state? Since there is no criterion to tell the difference, might you not be dreaming now? (3) Finally, suppose there is an evil genius so powerful and so evil that his main goal is to deceive you not just about your physical senses and your bodily states, but about everything, including $2 + 2 = 4$ and other mathematical and logical truths. Could it be that you are deceived about everything? Once Descartes moves us through these stages, he asks, what do we (still) know?

LIFE IN THE MATRIX

"I think, therefore I am." That's what we know. Not even the evil genius can deceive us about that, for to do so, he would have to convince us that we weren't having thoughts. But I can only think, "I'm deceived" or "I'm not having thoughts" if I am thinking. Since I am thinking, I exist. At this point, Descartes thinks we can return to the question, what is there? Well, at the very least, I am a thinking thing. Hence begins the notion of the autonomous thinker, free of all constraints but reason itself. Descartes's notion of reality thus begins with himself—his thinking, unemotional, disembodied self. He then argues for the existence of God (who won't deceive us, since God is perfect and good) and then to the existence of his body and back to the so-called "external world," the world outside his own thoughts.

The important thing to remember here is the following shift. Up until the modern era, most people thought of the human person as part of the rough and tumble of the world, as a being who knows about the world (and maybe God) first, and only later about herself. With the beginnings of modernity people began to think: I know about myself (and only myself) first, and then about God and the world (or the world and God). Another important thing is that with the modern era, the question of knowledge became more important than the question of what there is. Now if Descartes had been right, perhaps all would have been well and good. Unfortunately, virtually everyone thinks Descartes's arguments for the existence of God and the external world are problematic. Certainly, in Western culture his arguments for God have often been rejected. There is also a deep problem with the criteria Descartes sets out for what counts as knowledge. We won't go into it here, but it's called the Cartesian circle. The title alone might suggest to you some circular reasoning—that is, assuming what you are trying to show. We'll leave it at that. So if Descartes's arguments are not valid, how does he (or we or I) get outside his own thoughts? Perhaps all that exists is a person and her thoughts. A deep skepticism is set free to roam the world (that is, if there is a world!).

Perhaps a brief autobiographical note here might help. When Mark first took a philosophy class in the mid-1970s, he read Descartes. Mark loved what Descartes had to say. So Mark sat down to write his own apologetic for the faith. He tried, not very elegantly but very earnestly, to capture what Descartes said in Mark's own words. He followed the skeptical arguments out, and then set out on the path of reconstruction. He didn't get very far. He still has the notebook in which he tried this approach. It ends abruptly at the move to the external world. He rather liked Descartes's argument for God, but he couldn't see how a person could know that God would guarantee his knowledge of things outside himself. (Remember, for Descartes, human reason more or less rules supreme, and in particular, the individual, isolated human reason.) After all, his own reason was supposed to be the judge. God's existence wasn't all that clear, and even if it was, Mark knew that, like all human beings, he regularly made mistakes in judgment. This early foray into philosophical writing and thinking set Mark into a decade of deep skepticism about the nature of the world and, eventually, into skepticism (again) about how humans could know about God. Yet all through this period in Mark's life, he always thought there was a solution to these problems, if only he could think hard enough. The world, he thought, was a unity. Mark's experience with Descartes matches that of many philosophers in the modern age—they are captured by Descartes's vision of how to do philosophy (start with epistemology and the isolated mind), but they are frustrated by their inability to push Descartes's project through to a successful conclusion, and still they believe deep down that the world makes sense. In a postmodern age, fewer and fewer people still have that basic belief that the world is a unity.

LOCKE

Returning now to our philosophical history, we need to note that philosophy took two routes during the modern period. On the continent of Europe, Descartes was an early thinker in what is called "rationalism." Many others followed him, the two most important of whom were Spinoza and Leibniz. Like Descartes, they both thought reason could give us answers about the "external world." We are going to pass over these thinkers to talk about the other important route, which largely developed in the small but powerful islands we now think of as Great Britain. The three thinkers we will talk about here are John Locke, Bishop George Berkeley, and David Hume. These, and those who follow in the tradition flowing from their work, are called "empiricists" because of their emphasis on the source of knowledge being our five senses rather than reason alone. Each one, however, is influenced by Descartes's shift to knowledge first.

In attempting to answer the question of how we know about the world outside the individual mind, Locke proposed that the human mind receives information about, let's say, the book in front of you, via the five senses. You see the book, touch the book, smell the book (if you get close enough), and hear the book (let's say, when it drops), or taste the book (if you are so bold!). The data from the book is then received or impressed on your mind and you get an "image" of the book in your mind. That image, when it matches the reality of the book, is a true image and we can have, thus, true beliefs. Locke assumed that the external world (the world outside our thoughts) was real and that our mental images of it could match the world when our senses and reason were operating properly. Of course, some things about the world outside the mind are dependent on us rather than the world. For example, how warm the room feels to an individual is a subjective thing. Color, too, is subjective; otherwise a person with color blindness would not see a different color than someone without color blindness. So there are objective properties (Locke called them "primary qualities") and subjective ones ("secondary qualities"). Properties are, for our purposes, the way things are. Trees have the property of having leaves. Tables have the property of having more or less flat surfaces on the top. Cows have the property of being four-legged. And so forth. Properties were thought, by Locke (and by most of us!) to continue whether we are perceiving the object or not. At least, that's what Locke thought about primary or objective properties. The tree has leaves even when we are not looking. Of course, we can see how we might be more skeptical about whether the leaves are green, since the greenness seems to depend on someone *experiencing* greenness.

BERKELEY

Bishop George Berkeley came along, however, and noted that the reasons for the distinction between objective and subjective aspects of the world are not as good as they seem. Why? Locke assumed that the world is real and "out there." Berkeley argued that, in fact, *all* properties are subjective or secondary. Hence, in order for something to be what it is, that thing must be perceived. Some thought will show that if Berkeley is correct, then just as the warmth or coolness of the room is subjective (that is, internal only to my experience) so is the room itself! If someone isn't here to experience the room, the room doesn't exist. Berkeley's motto is "to be is to be perceived." Fortunately for our common sense, Berkeley was a Christian (as were Locke and Descartes) and he thought that God, who never sleeps nor slumbers, is always perceiving the room and, in fact, all of creation, so rooms do not pop in and out of existence depending upon whether some human is in them! So Berkeley doesn't fundamentally doubt that properties continue to be over time. The leaves I look at now as I peer out my front window are the same leaves I looked at five minutes ago when I was peering through the same window. God, the Great Perceiver, guarantees it. It is fair to say that not many people have been persuaded by Berkeley's overall position, but it is an important step in the historical story.

HUME

Enter David Hume. Hume's heritage for us is both skeptical and naturalistic. We will go into some detail in the next chapter on the nature of modern naturalism, but Hume had an important influence on how it developed. He rejected the arguments for God's existence, along with, potentially, any truly meaningful talk about the way God really is. That is why Hume was a *naturalist*; he did not believe in God, immaterial souls, or anything whose existence could not be confirmed empirically. But Hume is classed as a *skeptic* because his disbelief went much farther; Hume's skepticism did not extend merely to God but to what we can know about the natural world. Hume, building on the work of Locke and Berkeley, noted that, in the end, all experience of the world is subjective to the human person. Even Berkeley's arguments for the collapse of the objective (primary) properties into the subjective (secondary) properties is faulty because, Hume thought, the notion that there are properties that continue over time is faulty. While Berkeley believed there were tables we experience, or at least the brownness or solidity of a table, Hume said no. All we experience is the immediate data itself. I look at the table at 4:00 p.m. and it appears to be a brown table. I look at 4:05 p.m. and it appears again to be a brown table. But why think it is the same table? For that matter, what makes it the same brownness? All I have is my immediate experience. (Remember, the source of all my information about the external world is derived from my five senses.) All I have is brown, here, now. When I close my eyes and open them again, I have brown, here, now. But why think there is an underlying brownness, let alone an underlying tableness?

Hume also wondered about the very ground of science. For example, if all I have is my experience, what makes me think the future will be like the past? In the past the sun has always risen in the East. (Of course, we know that is only an appearance, since the sun isn't rising but the planet is turning . . . but let's not worry about that!) However, just because it always happened in the past, it doesn't follow that it will happen tomorrow. For all I know, tomorrow could be fundamentally different from the past, and *all* my experience has been experience of the past. I have exactly zero experience relevant to the future. Hume also questioned "cause and effect," the idea that one event causes another. Suppose you watch a soccer ball being kicked by a friend of yours. You see her foot connect with the ball. You see the ball move. You assume that the movement of her foot—its force, its motion, etc.—causes the ball to move. But can you actually see cause and effect? Or do you simply see one event (the moving foot touching the ball) and a second event (the ball moving away from the foot)? Why assume that cause and effect is in the two events? Your five senses alone can't tell you. The very basis for science is shaky.

One more thing about Hume. When he asked questions about the human self, he wondered if we have good evidence for a self that exists through time. Here is an experiment you can try, remembering that for Hume and the empiricists more generally, all that exists is what we have experience of via the five senses. Close your eyes and sit still for a minute. "Look" inside yourself. Can you experience your "self"? Don't you just get a flood of ideas—images, thoughts, emotions, etc.? Can you see *yourself* in there? Aren't you, according to Hume's criteria, just a bunch of more or less random thoughts, what Hume called a "bundle of impressions"? What is the human self?

Hume's answers to the many questions he raises focus on what we might call psychological responses. The fact that we expect the future to be like the past, or the desk to still be brown when we open our eyes, is just a psychological mechanism based on what Hume called "constant conjunction." In the past, every time I let a stone free from my hand, it has fallen down. So I become accustomed to a connection between the past and the future, cause and effect. But the important point here is that there are no rational (only psychological) grounds for this belief. After Hume, the idea of an essence looks to be in pretty bad shape. But Hume is still working in a Cartesian framework: what is rational is disembodied, nonemotional thinking. Hume just doesn't think human beings have much reason to think they are essentially rational beings; in fact, they aren't essentially anything.

KANT

Hume says, at one point, that when these questions are too much for him, he goes out and plays backgammon. Today he might have played a video game to distract himself. But we're not so sure that is the best approach. Immanuel Kant certainly did not think so. He is perhaps the most important philosophical character in shaping the contemporary cultural world of the West. Kant is also known for the difficulty of his writing and his ideas. So we will try, on the one hand, to make his thoughts clear while at the same time not getting him wrong. Here goes.

Let's start with what Kant thought was at stake. Hume's thoughts about empiricism and where they led were, Kant thought, exactly right. If we begin with the notion that humans passively receive information from the external world and that the five senses are the sole means of receiving that information, Hume appears to be correct. That the future is going to be like the past is questionable. That cause and effect is in the physical world also looks to be unfounded. Kant's radical solution to this set of problems was to change the rules of the game. Instead of looking for cause and effect, for example, out there in the world, why not look inside ourselves? In fact, why assume that humans simply take a passive role in receiving information from the universe? Why not understand humans as taking an active role? Why not put cause and effect in us rather than trying to find it out there? This, for Kant, is not just psychologizing, as we found in Hume.

This may also sound a little like Berkeley, but it's not. It is very important to understand that Berkeley was an empiricist. Kant was not. He was a new sort of philosopher. Berkeley thought that the world is dependent on us. The world just *is* a collection of our experiences (or, more exactly, God's experiences). But we do not actively contribute to the world. We just receive experiences. Kant's view is much stronger and shifts the ground. We actually contribute to the nature of the world.

Here some pictures might help. First, the empiricists:

Locke:

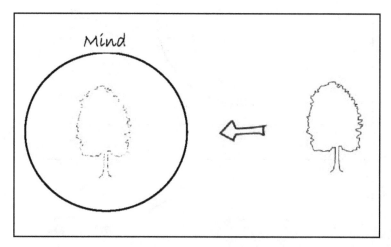

Berkeley:

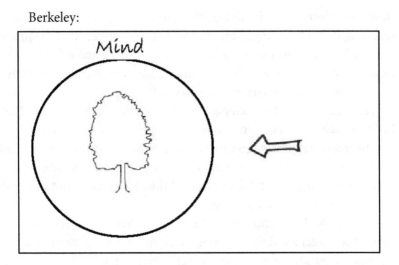

Hume:

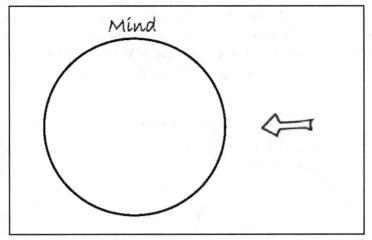

Kant:

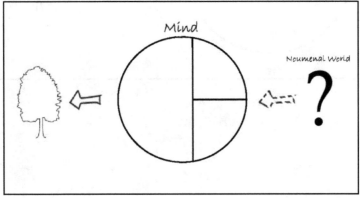

In Kant's understanding of the world, we don't know how the world is in and of itself. What he calls the noumenal world—the way things really are—is beyond us. All we have contact with is the phenomenal world, the world of experience. But we can experience the world only if it is shaped and molded by us. For the empiricists like Hume, we passively receive the world. For Kant, we actively make it. (This is somewhat overstated, for Kant thought there were important "limits" on our experience. Remember, we are merely attempting a sort of cultural survey.)

Let's take cause and effect. We know from Hume that we can't get cause and effect out of observation. Kant revolutionized the way we think about cause and effect by claiming that cause and effect of structures are brought *to the world* via the human mind. The human mind—the rational mind—is the same everywhere in terms of its basic contribution to the experienced world. So we all experience the same world, according to Kant, since we all have the same rational structure of the mind, a structure which then shapes and makes the world the way it is. Kant's solution to the empiricist challenge is simply to place the really important stuff in the mind. Humans thus know the phenomenal world (emphasis on the *phenomenal*) because we give it structure via rationality. But the world as it really is—the world in itself, the noumenal world—we don't know and, indeed, can't know. So Kant solves the problem of the external world by making it the world of appearance and not the world as it is independent of any human contribution.

Kant thought his proposal worked well for science and the physical world—the world of cause and effect and deterministic comings and goings. But it didn't work so well for ethics and religion. For these he proposes alternative ways of thinking. What is of particular interest for us is that Kant believed deeply in human free will but found it incompatible with his account of physics and the sort of reasoning by which he grounded physics. Cause and effect are deterministic. Freedom is not. So for Kant human free will is a posit, a sort of assumption needed to make sense out of our moral lives. But it doesn't rest on pure reason. Likewise God is a posit—something we need to make meaning in our lives. Yet, we certainly cannot appeal to the physical world in order to show that God exists. The physical world is the world of cause and effect. God, not falling under the categories via which we experience the world, cannot be yet another cause. Arguments for God's existence are thus thought not to work. God and ethics and beauty—the things that make for a meaningful human life—fall outside the realm of pure reason. Kant thought we have practical reasons to believe in God and other such things, but they are, strictly speaking, *unknowable* on the sort of grounds by which we know things about the physical world. The long-searched for unity underlying human meaningfulness and flourishing is substantially weakened by Kant's approach.

Furthermore, one of Kant's main assumptions was that the rational, human mind is, in fact, the same everywhere. But how do we know that? Why think the way one of us conceives the world is the same as the way others do? Kant is a preeminent Enlightenment and modern figure. Reason rules all, and where else should we begin but with our own reason? But the modern person, and Kant is no exception, makes a big assumption in taking the human person to be a free-standing, thinking entity. In Kant, in a way, essences are embedded in *human* existence and thought.

While there is a great deal more to Kant, we will have to settle for just a few cultural observations about the results of the Enlightenment. People believed in progress and reason. If we can just think clearly enough and hard enough, if we can just educate people, we will be able to solve our problems. The late nineteenth century in Europe was a time, in some ways, of great tolerance and openness. Yet shortly after the turn of the twentieth century, much of Europe was engaged in two terrible world wars, one of which led to the slaughter of six million innocent people simply because of their cultural and religious heritage. Jews and Gypsies were rounded up, forced into terrible labor camps, and then worked to death or killed outright. What happened to the tolerance of the Enlightenment and its overall structure rooted in modernity?

EXISTENTIALISM

Instead of replying to that question, we want to turn to the philosophical response to the twentieth century and its terrible wars. One response was that of existentialism. Rather than talk about existentialism in general, we'll talk about one of its representatives, Albert Camus. (One of the charms of existentialism is that it is not really a school or even a movement but a loosely connected set of ideas held by quite different and frequently disagreeing thinkers.)

Camus's "The Myth of Sisyphus" describes the ancient drama of Sisyphus. Sisyphus, a mortal, challenges his wife. He tells her that upon his death, she is to dispose of his body by throwing it out in the street rather than by a proper burial. When Sisyphus dies, his wife must choose. Should she obey Sisyphus's command and throw his body into the street and thus do a despicable thing, or bury him properly, honor his memory, and thereby disobey him? She threw his body out into the street.

Sisyphus, meanwhile, is in the underworld. He convinces the god Hades to release him to chastise his wife, who had dishonored him. Hades agrees. But once freed from the darkness of the underworld, once feeling the sun on his cheeks and the wind in his face, Sisyphus runs away from his death. Hades is not happy. He spends a lot of time chasing Sisyphus down. Once captured, Sisyphus is returned to the underworld. But instead of the chance at advancing to the Elysian Fields where the righteous dead go, Sisyphus is given an eternal punishment. Each day he is to roll a large rock to the top of a hill. At the end of the day, the rock rolls back down to the bottom and Sisyphus returns to roll it up again the next day.

For Camus, the fate of Sisyphus is the fate of the human person. We are bound to the rock we must roll, day after day, up again to the top of the hill, only to have it return that evening to the bottom. Our lives are mundane, repetitive and boring. Life is, indeed, absurd. So the main question of Camus's "The Myth of Sisyphus" is whether suicide is moral, given the absurdity of modern existence. His answer, in brief, is no. Suicide is not moral, but Camus supplies a rather strange reason. Suicide is not moral because it will decrease the number of experiences a person can have.

Lest that seem a rather weak reason, it is important to consider another aspect of existentialist thought, namely, that we humans are free in very radical ways. One way to put this point is to recall the original notion of essence (what a person truly is) preceding existence (the particulars of a person's life), a framework assumption of Western culture up until the twentieth century. With the existentialists, the formula is reversed. Existence precedes essence. With Camus and other secular existentialists (there are Christian existentialists too—Søren Kierkegaard, Paul Tillich, and perhaps Gabriel Marcel), there is no God to make us. We are "thrown" into the world. We have no essence but we exist first (hence the name, "existentialist") and then we are free to make up our own essence.

We want to connect this last point to something you read earlier. Kant thought we "make-up" the world and find freedom outside the structures of pure reason. Freedom was a posit for Kant, an assumption. Yet Kant thought humans had a shared nature, an essence in virtue of which all rationality was the same and which ultimately rooted our ethical lives. Once we arrive in the twentieth century, once God is removed from the realm of the rational, philosophers faced a crisis. Given the inexorable laws of nature, the mechanical cause and effect of the natural order, how do we explain freedom and morals and beauty? For the existentialist, freedom is assumed, but it is radically removed from what we think of as the realm of knowledge and world. It is completely subjectivized. Any person's nature just is what she can make of herself. No one has any essence but the one she makes up. We don't share an essence. There are no Platonic essences out there, no God creating human commonalities. There are just the mechanisms of the natural order (the rolling of the rock up that hill only to watch it roll down again) or the chaos of freedom (the ability, in Camus, to embrace the absurdity of a Sisyphean life). The seeds of this are in Kant, and even in Descartes, but the plant has grown to maturity in the existentialist movement.

POSTMODERNISM

Most of the readers of this book are not existentialists. You are, instead, postmoderns. What's the difference? The existentialists had not escaped the "I" of Descartes. It is arguable that postmoderns have. Furthermore, the existentialists hadn't quite given up the thought (although they tried!) that humans everywhere think alike, that the rational structures of the human mind are the same for all peoples, for all cultures. Postmodernism clearly leaves the modern assumptions of Descartes, Hume, Locke, and Kant behind. Imagine humans as individuals being responsible not only for themselves (as the existentialist would have) but for the creation of the whole world too! There is no reason, says the postmodern, to think we all create the world the same way. This is not "existence precedes essence" (a slogan of some existentialists) but simply "existence." Yet even existence is not something some versions of postmodernism can talk about. The very structures of existence and rationality become, in some sense, totally fictionalized.

So we finally arrive at the main point. Congratulations for making it this far! We think our audience—that is, people born after or around the early to mid-1980s (of course, not only folks from this age group, but that's who we are aiming at)—no longer believe in a unity underlying human nature or, for that matter, nature itself. There is no basic touchstone, no integrating factor bringing everything together. We can illustrate by returning to the story we told at the very beginning of this chapter where we wanted you to imagine yourself sitting in a class lecture about porcine insulin production. We said that you might be wondering what porcine insulin, intellectual property rights, philosophy, religion, the Bible and truth-telling all have to do with each other. For a postmodern, the answer is: very little or nothing! Postmoderns live, we think, in very different worlds. What we mean is that at any given time a postmodern lives in one frame of reference and then later in another. Sometimes these worlds or reference frames overlap in time and content, but often there is little obvious connection between them. We think this is due, in part, to the cultural results of the history of ideas just surveyed.

For our imagined student from the first paragraph, one world is sitting in class, listening to the instructor who, presumably, knows what he or she is talking about. Let's call it the world of biological education. In this world there is empirical information to gather about insulin, pigs, and the connection between porcine insulin and human insulin, as well as the connection to diabetes. Perhaps there is, in general, the concern of the instructor to communicate how God's world works, and the value of basic biological knowledge to living your life. A second world is the web-world, via which information relevant directly to the class can be gathered. The world of the text message creeps in too, in this case, where one ignores the immediate context of the biological education world and its rules of etiquette or perhaps morality (paying attention to the one speaking, taking seriously the presence of the other person, learning all one can so as to improve oneself) to avail oneself of a chuckle. It is the (partial) equivalent of passing notes in class but perhaps much more insidious. Inside the web-world, there is yet other world—or many worlds. One leaps from topic to topic (the meaning of "porcine," porcine philosophy and religion, a book, a new topic—intellectual property rights). The world of the ethics class emerges as well, one in which other important topics are introduced but which do not bear directly on the subject of biological education. The social world in which you are physically but not spiritually or mentally present contrasts with your own mental world, including the thought that it's not clear whether one needs to share one's thoughts with another person. Do you need to tell the truth? Is there yet another world, the world of ethical behavior or character development? And then there is the world of the Bible study which seems to indicate that one's tongue can do great evil, a world that sets you up for not preparing for the biological education world in which you now sit. (Perhaps, though, it was that third cup of coffee after the Bible study, the one where you started to talk with that good-looking woman or man sitting across the room from you!)

People have always lived with distractions and struggled with bringing together various aspects of their lives. The difference, we think, in our current culture is the underlying assumption that these various subjects and aspects seem *disconnected* at some deep level. As we noted above, in our postmodern situation, many of us wonder if everyone's rationality is the same. There may be a kind of rationality for women and a different one for men, one for Asian students, another for Westerns, one for the Thai student, another for the black South African. Perhaps, in fact, there is a different rationality and hence a different reality for each of these groups. Perhaps, indeed, there are different rationalities and realities for each individual. Finally, within one's own life, perhaps there are different realities—worlds or frames of reference—one moves in and out of. With a postmodern worldview, it seems as if people have achieved the "self" that Hume thought we all have—no self at all. Perhaps there are simply no connections between and among the various worlds. What, then, is the point of trying to see integrative connection or trying to grasp some illusive unity? There simply is, we postmoderns are tempted to think, no unity in the first place. Our religious lives (Bible study) are not connected to our moral lives (the temptation to lie) or to our biological education lives (the study of diabetics and insulin production) or to the various lives we enter through the worlds of the web and texting each other. Any given world seems to be as important as each of the others and all equally real or, perhaps, not real at all.

One of the very odd things about the postmodern situation is that even while we are postmodern, we can slip into and live in a modern world. This is partly due to the influence of Kant, who tended to radically separate the realms of science on the one hand from morality, religion, and aesthetics on the other. Naturalism, which we discuss in the next chapter, is one aspect of the heritage of the modern worldview. Postmodernism would point us toward the position that each and every one of the worlds in which we live is just as real or as valuable or as important as the others. At least sometimes, one of our worlds is the world that says that each of us is a totally autonomous thinking entity. (Note in the example from the earliest paragraphs of this chapter, the moment in which one thinks: "Do I have to share my thoughts with this other person?") The modern world is thus embedded in the postmodern worlds in which we live as one alternative reality, one where I am all alone and the sole arbiter of truth. Perhaps, too, it is a world in which we see the apparent mechanisms of the physical world working away, free of moral, religious, or aesthetic concerns or realities.

We want to challenge certain facets of the postmodern situation. Not all of them! We are certainly not opposed to everything in postmodernism. Yet we don't accept postmodernism whole-hog (to keep with our porcine theme!). In particular we want to challenge the apparent division among different realities in one's own life. We want to challenge *personal* lack of unity. Since we think unity is needed for integration, for flourishing, it is vital to retain a unity across worlds.

But before we leave this chapter, we want to return briefly to talk about doubt. Both of your authors mentioned that we faced doubt about our Christian commitments during our youth. We think perhaps our doubt might be a little different than the sorts of doubts facing postmodern youth. We think it is important enough to reflect on those differences at least for a while.

There are different kinds of doubt. There is doubting that something is true. There is doubting in the sense that one believes something but can't or doesn't really live out what one says. There is doubt brought about by ambiguity—you think you believe one thing but it turns out that you really believed something else that merely sounded like the thing you thought you believed. You can doubt what someone says not because you have independent reasons for disbelieving it, but because you don't trust the speaker. We think postmodern doubt may be different in some ways from all the above. We think postmodern doubt is less about thinking something false and more like thinking that everything is made up. It's sort of like discovering that Santa Claus isn't real. The presents are real, the celebration is real, your family is real, but the main character in your experience of Christmas isn't real. You see cardboard cutouts of Santa, Santa lit up on many roofs in your neighborhood, and Santa in the local shopping mall. But you know that there is no real Santa. It's all a sort of elaborate plot to sell toys.

Postmodern doubt is like finding out that *everything* is like Santa. There are pictures and poems and stories and jokes but nothing beyond them. Modern doubt was not like that. Modern doubt was like finding out that merely a slice of the story isn't true. One could always fall back on naturalism. Postmodernism leaves none of our big narratives with any truth at all. They are pure fiction. Perhaps, in fact, our own selves are pure fiction.

Postmodern doubt can leave one feeling completely empty. In modern doubt, one could keep looking for something to give meaning to one's life. Postmodern doubt leaves one wondering if there is any point at all. So we live our lives as if they are meaningless or perhaps just frivolous.

What we want to propose for your consideration is that doubt can also be a great opportunity. We think the idea that our lives, whether corporate or individual, are meaningless or perhaps just frivolous is either just wrong or at least a poor way to think and live. We may not be able to get to the truth of the matter. But we can still live with the hope that there *is* a truth of the matter. So we encourage our readers to live in hope, for hope sets up doubt as opportunity. Hope, we believe, goes hand in hand with our deep human sense of mystery.

3

Mystery and Naturalism: Entertaining Doubts About Modern Naturalism

Synopsis: A philosophical position called modern naturalism tries to banish mystery from the world. We validate our readers' experiences of mystery by introducing five reasons to be suspicious of modern naturalism. Once a reader entertains doubts about modern naturalism, the door to mystery is open.

W E THINK MOST OF our readers are already familiar with a worldview we will call "modern naturalism." We call it "modern" because this worldview emerged in the period of modern philosophy. Remember, that's roughly 1650–1950, so some of the main ideas of modern naturalism have been influential in our culture for a couple hundred years.

Remember again, from chapter 1: a worldview draws together ideas about reality, knowledge, and value. It gives us a background for all our beliefs and decisions.

MODERN NATURALISM

Modern naturalism is not just one idea, but several ideas combined into a comprehensive worldview. We will limit our discussion in this chapter to just a few of the main ideas of modern naturalism. Perceptive readers will undoubtedly be able to supplement what we say here; you will be able to think of other important parts of the modern naturalist worldview. Perhaps you will also think of reasons to doubt the modern naturalist worldview beyond those we suggest.

The most important tenet of modern naturalism is that the natural world simply *is* the world. According to the modern naturalist, if anything is real, it must be part of the natural world. There is no God as the Jews, Christians and Muslims imagine, for they think God exists "outside" the natural world. These religions teach that God is "supernatural." According to modern naturalism, the very idea of something outside of nature or above nature is nonsense. Nature simply *equals* all that exists.

Modern naturalism is certain that there is no God, and it is just as certain that there are no gods. By "gods" we mean spiritual forces or beings that supposedly exist as part of the universe. There are certainly no angels, demons, *avataras*, *bodhisattvas*, *kuei-shen*, or the like. Modern naturalism says there may indeed be creatures in the universe about which we know nothing, but such creatures would be extra-terrestrials, physical beings from other planets, not spiritual beings that somehow inhabit this planet. The only "gods" that might be real would be extraterrestrials who use advanced technology to hide their presence from us. In the modern naturalist worldview, science fiction aliens are *possible*, even if they are extremely unlikely. But the gods, angels, and demons as traditionally conceived in the religions cannot be real.

The second feature of modern naturalism is that *science* teaches us about the natural world. In practice, this functions as a definition of what "nature" is; the natural world just is whatever science studies. As a pure definition it's not very good, because it's circular: science studies the natural world, and the natural world is whatever science studies. In practice, however, the definition works well enough, because "science" can be identified sociologically. There are millions of scientists in the world, and they spend much of their time (and lots of money) doing scientific research. In a rough and ready way, the scientists of the world discipline each other. They have ways of praising and rewarding certain kinds of scientific activity while discouraging and excluding pseudo-science. So the modern naturalist is not committed to approving everything that every so-called scientist teaches about the world. Over time, good science will correct the errors of bad science, and humanity will gradually learn the truth about the universe.

Science works, the modern naturalist emphasizes, because it is thoroughly and steadfastly empirical. Science produces theories to explain empirical evidence, and it judges those theories by means of further sensory observations.[1] The data set of science does not include religious beliefs or mythologies, except in the limited sense that social scientists ought to explain how human beings have at various times created and passed on such beliefs. Large areas of human feeling—art, religion, love, ethics—may certainly be studied scientifically, but it is clear from the outset that the social sciences will teach us only about human beings and human culture. Our feelings and spiritual experiences tell us about ourselves, not about the universe.

Because science progresses over time, the modern naturalist believes in the goal of a "completed science." The actual words "completed science" probably show up most often in textbooks devoted to philosophy of science, but the idea of a completed science is widespread. A completed science is a scientific discipline (biology, chemistry, or whatever) not as it is understood now, but as it will be understood sometime in the distant future. Scientists' current beliefs about biology, to take an example, will undoubtedly be modified as biologists make new discoveries. So when modern naturalism says that the natural world simply is the real world, it means the natural world as it will be understood in the future.

A third feature of the modern naturalist worldview is this. Even though our current scientific beliefs are not perfect, enough of the outline of completed science has been already discovered to give us a pretty good picture of how human beings fit into the natural order. The outline goes something like this: as a species, *Homo sapiens* is a fairly recent product of evolution, appearing on the world stage in the last few million years. Evolution works by means of random genetic changes plus natural selection; there is no purpose or "guiding hand" in evolution. There is no sense in which the long history of evolution on our planet *intended* to produce human beings or any other species. Natural selection rewards those species whose genetic make-up allows them to reproduce; the others are eliminated. Religious views that give humanity a place of special honor or status in the universe—as if God made the universe for our benefit or created us with special dignity—are simply false. Our species

---

1. Actually, scientists judge their theories according to several criteria, including predictiveness, explanatory power, simplicity, and beauty. Many philosophers of science have pointed out that these criteria cannot all be reduced to empirical adequacy. But all philosophers of science will at least agree that empirical adequacy is one important criterion of theory choice.

is merely one species among many. It is true that we have an adaptive capacity, our intelligence, that has enabled us to achieve astounding reproductive success, especially in the last three hundred years. However, in the long term it is not yet clear that intelligence is the most successful evolutionary strategy; we have invented various technologies that give us the power to destroy the environment that sustains us. We could, by means of bombs or super-germs or climate change, eliminate our own species. In terms of natural selection, cockroaches could still be the "winners."

Human behavior and human thinking have arisen, just as all animal behavior and thinking have arisen, as adaptations to natural environments. Many modern naturalists think determinism must be true, though some of them still hope to reconcile belief in free will with neurobiology. (Determinism is the doctrine that all events, including human choices, are caused by prior events. There is no free will.) On that question, we still don't know enough; we are waiting for a more complete science.

A fourth feature of modern naturalism is its belief in the hierarchy of the sciences. The idea here is that the various sciences are interrelated and that more complicated or complex things are to be explained in terms of simpler things. For example: social phenomena, which involve groups of people, can be explained in terms of individual people; so sociology is reducible to psychology. The resulting hierarchy of the sciences is a familiar modern naturalist idea:

Social Sciences (Economics, Sociology, Political Science)
↑
Psychology
↑
Biology (including Neurobiology)
↑
Chemistry
↑
Physics

The list just given focuses on human beings, putting social sciences at the top. If we were interested in a different part of nature, say a forest, it might look like this:

Ecology
(the study of the relationships between species and environment)
↑
Biology
↑
Earth Sciences
(Geology, Hydrology, Cosmology)
↑
Chemistry
↑
Physics

The hierarchy of the sciences helps explain why in the twentieth century physics was accorded superlative respect among the sciences. In the end (that is, when the sciences are complete) everything will be explained in terms of physics. The "theory of everything" that some scientists hope to devise will be a theory in physics. Technological developments (for instance, nuclear weapons) also seemed to underscore the importance of physics.

To many people with modern naturalist worldviews, the hierarchy of the sciences implies reductionism. This is the idea that chemistry really is nothing but physics, biology is nothing but chemistry, and so on all the way up the hierarchy. As with determinism, some modern naturalists don't like reductionism and try to avoid it. They would say it is still an open question whether the higher sciences really are reducible to the lower ones.

MODERN NATURALISM AND THE GOD OF THE GAPS

Several times over the last couple centuries, some people have criticized the emerging modern naturalist worldview by pointing to holes in then-current scientific theories. For instance, some objected to the theory of evolution by asking why we do not find many transitional forms in the fossil record—i.e., where are all the "missing links"? Others went on to suggest that God intervened in the evolutionary process to help it along.

The evolution case is just an example. When we refer to the "God of the gaps" we mean any case in which God is introduced as an explanation for a hole in the current scientific picture of the universe. For example, it has been calculated that the observable mass of our galaxy (and presumably all the other galaxies) is not sufficient to correlate with the rotational speed of the galaxy. Suppose someone said: "Well that shows that God must exist. God is stepping in to assist the galaxies so that they can rotate properly without disintegrating." This would be to introduce a "God of the gaps." Now, we know of no one who has actually made this claim. The astrophysicists who are working on this problem have instead postulated that the observable masses of the galaxy (stars, interstellar gasses, etc.) actually make up only about 5% of the total mass of the galaxy. The rest of the galaxy is made up of "dark matter" that we can't see. Possibly, the dark matter of the galaxy consists of black holes whose gravity is so intense that they give off no light.

Modern naturalists emphatically reject appeals to any "God of the gaps." They willingly admit that our current scientific understanding of the universe is incomplete; they emphasize that we still have much to learn. But we have to look for answers in the right places. It makes sense to solve the galaxy rotation problem by reference to "dark matter" rather than by reference to God. "Dark matter," even though it sounds mysterious, is really a label for some natural phenomenon that we can explore scientifically, even if we don't yet know what natural phenomenon it is. The gods imagined by religious people are by definition mysterious and beyond scientific exploration.

This is a point we want to emphasize. *The modern naturalistic worldview is closed to mystery.* Modern naturalists eagerly admit that there are many things we don't know, but they insist that eventually science will fill in all the gaps. And we already know enough to have a good picture of the world. Reality is physical, mechanical, deterministic, and reductionistic (though some modern naturalists quibble about determinism and reductionism). Value judgments, both moral and aesthetic, must be understood as the judgments of the thinking animals that hold them. Love is something *we* feel. Beauty is something *we* see. Like all other human feelings or thoughts, these experiences are really nothing more than brain functioning (in conjunction with nervous system functioning, social interactions, etc.). In the end—when we have achieved a completed science—there will be nothing mysterious about the universe or our place in it.

WHAT DO WE MEAN BY "MYSTERY"?

We will invite our readers to be suspicious of the modern naturalist story. In particular, we invite you to be open to mystery, the deep mystery of human existence.

Ludwig Wittgenstein, one of the twentieth century's most enigmatic philosophers, once suggested that even if *all* scientific questions could be answered, people would still have the sense that the most important questions had not been addressed.[2] Wittgenstein himself seemed to think—at least for a while—this showed that the really important questions of human life could not be put into words. We think Wittgenstein was both right and wrong. He was right in that non-scientific questions are crucially important to human life. We think Wittgenstein was also right that the words we use to express the really deep questions are often inadequate; we have the feeling that our words only point in the general direction of mystery. However, we disagree with Wittgenstein's advice that we be silent about mystery. However inadequate human language is for the questions of mystery, we must ask them, and we invite readers to enter into the spirit of such questions. For instance:

- *Why does the universe exist? Why is there something rather than nothing?

- *Why does the "something"—the universe—contain life?

- *Why does the universe contain a particular life—mine?

- *How is it possible to recognize beauty?

- *What is love? What is cruelty?

- *What can I hope for?

- *What kind of life ought I live?

2. Wittgenstein, *Tractatus Logico-Philosophicus*, section 6.52.

SOME POOR REASONS TO BE SUSPICIOUS
OF MODERN NATURALISM

By this point in the chapter, some readers will realize that they *want* to *resist* the modern naturalist worldview. Perhaps they have had religious experiences of one sort or another, and they don't like the way modern naturalism discounts their experiences. (Usually, the modern naturalist will say that a religious *experience* is real enough, but it can be explained in terms of human psychology. The religious experience does not constitute evidence for the existence of gods.) Other readers will have had experiences of love or beauty, and they don't like to think of these experiences—those magical moments remembered as the best of our lives—as nothing but neurobiological events in their brains. Other readers believe deeply in free will—in particular, that they freely choose to do this or that—and they don't like the deterministic implications of modern naturalism.[3]

All this is fine. We applaud those of you, our readers, who resist the implications of modern naturalism. We don't like such implications either. But we need to be careful. *The fact that we don't like something doesn't make it false.* We need better reasons than our desires to question modern naturalism.

For example, it is true that current neurobiology cannot explain human consciousness. Some researchers in the field consider the problem of consciousness the most difficult scientific question today. Now, suppose someone were to say: "The brain scientists cannot explain my unified consciousness of my current visual field, including the cat, the water pot, and the painting on the wall.[4] They can't explain self-awareness, nor can they explain my free choices. So I reject modern naturalism, and I reject determinism."

This is still another example of the "God of the gaps." Instead of defending belief in God, it defends belief in free will (and self-awareness and unified consciousness). But the argument is the same. Because of a

3. Remember Kant, in chapter 2? Some people are attracted to Kant's philosophy because he limited science to the "phenomenal" world. In the 18th century Kant already could see that science was heading toward a mechanistic, deterministic worldview, but he said that even if that turned out to be true of the world of scientific study, the real "noumenal" world could still have beauty and free will.

4. "Unified consciousness" simply means that these different things are all part of one experience.

lack in current scientific understanding, it introduces *mystery*. (Free will, human choices that are undetermined by underlying physical reality, is fundamentally mysterious.) Modern naturalists can respond by saying that someday a completed neuroscience will explain consciousness and so-called free will. There is no reason to drag mystery into the universe, they will say, just because we don't currently understand it.

We invite our readers to be open to mystery and to be suspicious of modern naturalism, but we do not intend to appeal to current gaps in scientific theory. Instead, we will suggest five reasons that we think are based on *permanent* shortcomings in the modern naturalist worldview. We do not think future research will fix these problems. Of course, we may be wrong. It may turn out that one or more of these objections are really nothing more than "God of the gaps" problems. You, the reader, must judge for yourself. We are extremely confident that at least one or more of these five arguments will never be adequately answered by modern naturalism.

Let us be clear. We do *not* offer these objections as "proofs" for any religious belief, not even the belief that God exists. We offer them as reasons to be suspicious of the modern naturalist worldview. In much of the world today, the modern naturalist worldview is taken for granted. In many universities in America, for example, or in the state educational system of China, many people simply assume that modern naturalism must be true. Perhaps you are one of those people who have never questioned modern naturalism. We invite you to be open to mystery. Once you begin to doubt modern naturalism, perhaps you will be open to deeper mystery, including the mystery of human persons.

SOME GOOD REASONS TO BE SUSPICIOUS OF THE MODERN NATURALIST WORLDVIEW

First, the reductionistic and deterministic features of modern naturalism seem to be rooted in the physics of the nineteenth century, not the twentieth century. Why should we accept a worldview based on outdated science?

In a nineteenth-century view of the world, the universe is populated by big things like solar systems, which are composed of smaller things like planets and comets, which are composed of very small things like atoms. Somewhere in the mid-range of the scale we find living things like plants and animals. In this mechanical view of the universe, objects

act on each other through attraction (e.g. gravity or magnetism) or col-
lision. It is basically a billiard ball conception of things—objects bump
into each other. Fluids are made up of small particles that bump into
each other and slide by each other. Planets and comets orbit around stars,
their velocity balanced by the attraction of gravity. Occasionally a planet
or comet impacts another object, a large scale bumping. Every object,
whether large or small, has a location in space. The speed of the object
and its relations (attractions and collisions) with other objects will deter-
mine where it will be in the future. The universe is a giant machine with
the interactions of its parts governed by Newton's laws of motion. Surely,
the functioning of mid-sized machines such as animal bodies (including
human bodies, including human brains) is controlled by biological laws
and chemical laws, and those laws will turn out to be reducible to laws of
physics. Therefore, so-called free choices are illusions.

It is important to emphasize that the picture of the universe in
the previous paragraph is thoroughly out of date. Your authors are old
enough to remember school textbooks that pictured atoms as little solar
systems, with electron "planets" circling proton/neutron "stars." Even at
that time, scientists knew this picture was deeply misleading. That it was
still used testifies to the pervasive grip of the nineteenth-century view
of objects.

In the first third of the twentieth century, quantum dynamics
overturned the picture of the very small. According to the standard interpretation of quantum theory, first proposed by Werner Heisenberg,
an electron really is a probability, not a "thing" with a specifiable place
and velocity. Other scientists, including Albert Einstein and Erwin
Schrödinger, objected to Heisenberg's interpretation of the uncertainty
principle, but it has stood the test of time. Heisenberg's understanding
of quantum mechanics emphasizes the role of the *observer*, a human being outside of the quantum system being observed. Electrons (and other
particles) do not have a nature all on their own, so to speak, because
their nature is always revealed to be a function of measurement. At the
fundamental level, twentieth-century physics says that reality is partially
constructed by observation and thus observers.

Remember, we said that the objections we offer to modern naturalism are not just "gaps" problems. Someone might respond to this first
argument by saying that it is based on twentieth-century physics and
thus vulnerable to advances in the future. Maybe some physicist will

someday replace quantum dynamics with some better theory that will restore the ideal of pure objective location and motion in space-time. Well, that's possible. So maybe our first objection to modern naturalism is weak. Do you really think so?

Now, some people *resist* standard quantum dynamics, we suggest, because they want to believe the comforting, simple, billiard ball picture of nineteenth-century physics. They want to say: "The electron really has a speed and a location; we just can't measure it without affecting it." But remember what we said earlier about desires and beliefs: the fact that we would like something to be true doesn't make it true. Why should we hold so tightly to outdated conceptions? We suggest that standard quantum dynamics be taken at face value: electrons and other particles really are probability functions.

So here is our first statement of suspicion. Why should I accept modern naturalism's closed door if matter itself, at its core, is a probability function? It seems that *observers from outside the system being observed* are ineradicable in modern physics.

To be completely fair, we will point out that we have not proved that believers in modern naturalism are influenced by their desires for a comforting view of physics. We have merely asserted this. In a sense, our accusation is much like Marx's or Freud's assertions about the economic or psychological foundations of religious beliefs. You, the reader, will have to ask yourself: is it possible that I believe in nineteenth-century physics because I *want* to believe in that kind of world?

Second, how did the universe come to be? It seems clear that the universe did not always exist, that it came into being. Naturally, we want to ask how. But cosmology suggests that this question is permanently unanswerable. It is a mystery.

From Aristotle (fourth century BCE) until the early twentieth century, philosophers and scientists held that the physical universe might be eternal. Even the Christian philosopher Thomas Aquinas thought that we only know that God created the universe *in time* because the Bible says so. (Aquinas thought he could prove that God created the universe, but he thought God might have created the universe *eternally*.) Modern naturalists of the nineteenth and early twentieth centuries cherished this view that the universe is eternal. For all we know, they said, the physical universe has always existed. In this "steady state" view of the universe, new matter may come into existence, and old matter may disappear (how, we don't know, but someday we will find out), but the universe as a whole may very well have always been pretty much like it is now. We certainly don't need to believe in some mysterious God in order to explain the beginning of the universe if the universe didn't have a beginning!

One of the most readable and entertaining examples of this modern naturalist position is found in Bertrand Russell's *Why I am not a Christian.*[5] In this essay, Russell rejects out of hand the "first cause" argument (found in Aquinas and many other authors), which claims that God must exist as an explanation for the beginning of the universe. Russell's position was that the universe might very well have always existed. It's ironic that Russell published this famous essay in the late 1920s, at the same time that Edwin Hubble worked out the implications of some discoveries he made at the Mount Wilson Observatory in California. Hubble's findings destroyed the steady state theory of the universe. Most students today are familiar with Hubble's discoveries, but we should remember that they are less than a century old.

In 1922 through 1924, Hubble discovered that some stars are several hundred light years away, too distant to be part of our galaxy. For the first time, scientists realized that there are other galaxies in the universe. Then, in 1927, Hubble discovered something even more surprising: the other galaxies are all moving away from us. The universe is expanding. Hubble quickly realized that this means the universe was much smaller in the distant past.

Other scientists have corrected and refined Hubble's work since the 1920s. Current cosmology calculates that the Big Bang occurred about 13.7 billion years ago. Technically speaking, we cannot "rewind" the story of the universe back to the absolute beginning. At a barrier called Planck time (10^{-43} of the first second after the Big Bang) the universe would be smaller than a proton and the temperature would have exceeded 10^{32} degrees Kelvin. The physical laws of the universe as we know them would not apply. Space-time begins at Planck time. It is time zero, the beginning of space, the beginning of time. Words like "before" or "outside" do not apply to Planck time.

The natural universe—that is, the universe that physics can study—began at Planck time. (The word "after" *can* be properly used of Planck time; every event in the history of the universe came after Planck time.)

5. Russell, *Why I am not a Christian.*

So the modern naturalist picture of a steady state, eternal universe is no longer believable.

As in the case of quantum dynamics, some people *resist* the implications of Big Bang cosmology. An eternally existing physical universe is a comforting idea; it eliminates the mystery of a Creator. And so some philosophers and scientists proposed the "oscillating universe" theory to avoid the conclusion that the universe had a beginning. According to this model, the universe explodes and contracts repeatedly. There was never any evidence for this theory; it was motivated by philosophical desires. And then leading physicists Stephen Hawking and Roger Penrose showed that the gravity necessary for a "Big Crunch" would produce chaos, and the entropy would be too great to allow another explosion. It seems there is no getting round the fact that the universe started, just once.

Quite naturally, cosmologists and philosophers want to ask what caused the universe. But if there is a cause of the universe—something "outside" space or "before" time—science can't get at it. The cause of the universe is fundamentally mysterious. In the modern naturalist worldview, science studies the real world, and there is no place for mystery. But it seems our best theory in cosmology, the Big Bang theory, has reintroduced mystery in a big way. Is the existence of the universe a completely unexplainable brute fact? That strikes us as being as mysterious as any religious doctrine. *Why is there something rather than nothing?* Some of the religions take this question seriously and offer answers to it. It seems that modern naturalism recommends we ignore the question.

Third, the Big Bang gave us an extremely peculiar universe, a universe that strikes many scientists as being "finely tuned" to support life. How is it that we got so lucky?

Let us give a homespun illustration. Suppose a woman (call her Debbie) drives from her home in Los Angeles to Las Vegas to bet money at a casino. By the end of the weekend she has won $50,000, which she takes home to her bank. The casino owners will probably think nothing of it. Occasionally gamblers at casinos get lucky and win money. The casinos actually publicize such events, using them to lure new gamblers.

But suppose that Debbie returns to Las Vegas the next week and again wins $50,000. Now what would the casino owners think?

Suppose Debbie visits Las Vegas every week for a year. And every week she returns to Los Angeles and deposits $50,000 of gambling winnings in her bank account. We contend that, besides being very rich, Debbie would be in deep trouble. Why? Because the casino owners (and the Nevada Gaming Commission) do not believe that anyone could be that "lucky." Even though they might not have concrete proof, they would believe that Debbie was a cheater. They would watch Debbie's every move in order to discover how she was cheating them. Even if they couldn't catch her at it, they would warn her to stay away from Las Vegas. And if it were legally possible, they would forbid her to enter their casinos.

Why would the casinos be so sure that Debbie cheats? Because winning large amounts of money in games where the odds are stacked against the gambler is *improbable*, and winning repeatedly is far more improbable. At some point, the "lucky coincidences" of Debbie's gambling are so improbable that reasonable observers will insist that there must be some other explanation. As long as we have only one hypothesis, we will continue to think about whatever it is we are studying in terms of that hypothesis. But as soon as someone proposes an alternative hypothesis, we can compare and evaluate them. In this case, the "alternative hypothesis" generalizes from the common observation that some people try to cheat casinos. It's quite reasonable to believe that Debbie's string of gambling wins results from cheating rather than luck.

Enough of the illustration. We stress at this point that the improbability of the "lucky coincidences" in the fine-tuning argument is many orders of magnitude *greater* than the improbability of Debbie winning in Las Vegas every week for a year.

In the first microsecond after Planck time, the fundamental constants of our universe were established. Theoretically, each one of the constants could have had any of an almost infinite number of possible values. An illustration: think of an old-fashioned radio with an analog tuner knob. As you turn the knob right and left, the tuning indicator sweeps back and forth over that portion of the electromagnetic spectrum that the radio receiver can detect. If you stop the tuning indicator at the right place you can listen to a radio station broadcasting on that frequency. If you turn the knob too much or too little, you can't get the station. Each of the fundamental constants of the universe is like that; each value could have been set at any point among a wide spectrum of values.

In the universe we actually have, the strong nuclear force (which binds the particles of an atomic nucleus together) balances almost perfectly with the weak nuclear force (responsible for beta decay). If the strong force were weaker, atomic nuclei would not hold together, so hydrogen would be the only possible element. But if the strong force were only slightly stronger, hydrogen would be extremely rare, which would make stars (and thus all heavy elements) impossible. The strong force and the weak force had to be balanced (to a degree of exactness of one part in 10^{60}) for us to have a universe with plentiful hydrogen *and* the possibility of heavier elements.

Now imagine that you want to listen to a certain radio program, but you don't know the frequency of the radio station and you have to tune the radio in less than a second. Nor do you know what time of the day the program comes on. What are the chances of getting the program? The improbability of the strong force balancing the weak force is much greater than that.

But the weak force / strong force balance is just one example of fine-tuning. Another example: the explosive force of the Big Bang is balanced with the force of gravity—if gravity had been weaker, the universe would have had expanded faster and matter would be too spread out to form stars and planets, but if gravity had been stronger, the universe would have collapsed on itself long before stars could have formed.

The mind-boggling improbability of a long string of such "coincidences" has pushed some scientists and philosophers to believe that there must be some explanation other than luck. The universe appears to have been precisely tuned to produce conditions favorable to the evolution of life. Our universe has abundant hydrogen, long lived stars in which carbon and other heavy elements can form, stable star systems with planets of various sizes (and not too close to galaxy centers), and a long enough history between Planck time and the eventual heat death of the universe for life to emerge on some of the favored planets. How did we get so lucky?

If the oscillating universe model could work, we would have an answer. If there were an infinite number of universes appearing one after another, eventually every possible universe would appear in the sequence. Obviously, living beings (including intelligent living beings) would only exist in those universes that met all the qualifications for producing life. There would be no need for luck, no mystery. But Hawking and Penrose showed that the oscillating universe theory doesn't work, and modern naturalists have pretty much abandoned that idea in the last couple decades.

In recent years, some modern naturalists have proposed a different solution, the "multi-universe" model. This theory holds that many universes exist; in fact, some people have suggested that *every possible* universe exists. If the Big Bang produced not just this universe, but also an infinite number of universes, the fine-tuning problem goes away. Presumably, most of the universes are incredibly boring: gravity is too strong so they collapse in less than a second, or the strong force is too weak so hydrogen is the only element in the universe, or the strong force is too strong so the universe never produces enough hydrogen for a star (thus, never producing heavy elements), or any of an enormous number of lifeless universes. But in a few of the infinite array of universes in this model conditions would be right for life. And clearly, we must live in one of those few. No need for luck.

The multi-universe theory sounds attractive, until we recognize that it is entirely speculative. There is not, and by definition can never be, any evidence for it. If science could explore another universe, it would not be another universe, but part of this one. The multi-universe model is a philosophical theory, not a scientific theory; it is permanently untestable. Worse than that, from a modern naturalist point of view, it is *deeply mysterious*. It explains away the evidence for fine-tuning, but it does so by introducing an infinite number of universes about which we can know nothing. In spite of the mysterious character of the infinity of universes, some naturalists *prefer* the multi-universe theory to any religious view. This shows, we think, how belief in naturalism is rooted in philosophical desires, not science.

Why should we accept the modern naturalist's closed door against mystery when the finely tuned nature of our universe forces us to admit mystery?

Fourth, the one indispensable tool of science is mathematics. Since the modern naturalist worldview is closed to mystery, it would be extremely embarrassing if mystery were to turn up in mathematics. The modern naturalist worldview apparently assumes that there are no mysteries involved in math. There may be unsolved math problems, but no true mysteries. Once again, this seems to ignore developments in the twentieth century.

It's pretty clear that, on Earth, human beings are the only creatures to think up mathematical concepts. Some math concepts seem pretty straightforward, like whole integers; common human experiences, like counting, make it easy to understand how people acquired these ideas. Our students know that other math concepts are much less intuitive; it was a stroke of genius for Leibniz and Newton to invent calculus—and it is a challenge for students to learn it even today!

Mathematicians continue to think up new mathematical concepts; there is such a thing as mathematical research. Often, when the mathematicians have clarified a mathematical problem or come up with a new mathematical idea, theorists in the physical sciences take up that new concept and ask how it will help them explain problems in biology, chemistry, physics, and the like. For instance, graph theory was invented to solve basic recreational problems—like the "bridges of Konigsberg" (could a Konigsbergite cross every bridge in the city exactly once and end up in the section where she started?) and the "four color problem" (would a mapmaker ever need more than four colors?)—and then, 150 years later, computer scientists found a need for graph theory as they investigated sophisticated data storage problems.

Some philosophers have pointed out that such scientists operate on the basis of a fascinating assumption. They assume that the universe— no matter what part: subatomic, intergalactic, biological, etc.—can be properly described by math. The assumption implies that no matter how bizarre or chaotic the universe may appear, somehow underlying all the appearances there is a hidden order, and that order will be rational, and the rationality of the order will be mathematical. Now, this assumption is not just a modern assumption; some ancient and medieval philosophers also shared it. But when you think about it, it's a stunning bit of human confidence.

Someone might reply, "But our experience shows that math works. Our confidence is based on lots of success." True enough. But *why* does math work? What is it about the abstract thinking of a particular species on a particular planet that makes it such a wonderful tool for exploring the real universe?

There seems to be mystery in math—but the mystery gets deeper when we consider the relationship of math and logic. In 1911, Bertrand Russell and Alfred N. Whitehead published *Principia Mathematica*,[6] a

6. Whitehead and Russell, *Principia Mathematica*.

watershed event in the history of logic and math. Russell and Whitehead showed how to fuse math and logic. They presented a consistent system of symbolic logic that could be used to represent mathematical theorems. Very soon afterward, a philosopher/mathematician named David Hilbert challenged the mathematical community to go one step further. Mathematicians ought to show not only that math is a consistent axiomatic system; they ought to show that it is a complete system, one that could produce every true mathematical theorem (or at least every true theorem of arithmetic).[7] To many people's surprise, in 1931 Kurt Gödel proved that this was impossible. Gödel's proof shows that for every consistent axiomatic system of mathematics (Russell and Whitehead's system was merely the best system so far), there will be propositions that can neither be proved nor disproved in the system. Consider two implications of Gödel's result. First, there can never be any way to be sure that arithmetic does not contain contradictions, because all such all axiomatic systems, including arithmetic, have undecidable propositions. Second, even though Gödel's famous conclusion cannot be decided in the system, we human beings who are not in the system can see that it is true.[8] And if it is true, then it must be decidable by beings whose minds are not limited to an axiomatic system. Human beings have the ability to recognize mathematical truths that no mathematical system can produce.

Why should we accept a modern naturalist worldview, a worldview that says all the big questions will be eventually answered by science, when the most ubiquitous tool of science (mathematics) pushes open the door to mystery?

Fifth, it seems that the modern naturalist worldview logically undermines our confidence that our best theories might actually be true.

Remember that modern naturalism is eager to tell us something about our place in the universe. Religions sometimes imagine that human beings have a rather exalted place in the scheme of things, but modern naturalism emphasizes that our species is just one among many. Our planet is almost certainly only one of many planets. And so on. There is nothing all that special about us.

7. An axiomatic system starts with a limited number of assumptions (axioms) and uses a specific set of rules to produce logical conclusions. Think of geometry in middle school.

8. Roughly interpreted, Gödel's conclusion says, "This proposition can not be decided in the system of *Principia Mathematica*."

Remember also that we have evolved on this planet by means of chance (random genetic changes) plus natural selection. The universe did not intend to produce us. In a science fiction sense, it is possible that some alien species superintended our evolution (as in the movie, *2001: A Space Odyssey*), but no one really thinks it happened that way.[9]

We need to remind ourselves how natural selection works. Whenever some change in a species' physical make-up or behavior helps that species reproduce, that change will be passed on to future generations, provided that the change in physiology or behavior is encoded in genes. Only genetic inheritance counts.[10] If a particular animal enjoys a bountiful life, with lots of food, good health and many offspring, what does it pass on to those offspring? Only its genes, and the physiology and behavioral strategies encoded in those genes.

The physiology of the human brain, nervous system, and body somehow makes possible human intelligence. And human intelligence, especially when it is expressed in social cooperation (for instance, caring for and teaching children), has helped us pass on our genes. To date, it seems, natural selection has "approved" intelligence as a means of reproducing genes. (But don't forget that the cockroaches may outlast us.)

The theory of evolution thus teaches us that our genetic inheritance—including our physiology, intelligence, and our behavioral strategies—is a success, in so far as it has actually helped us pass on our genetic inheritance. This is true of every species. The genetic inheritance of the Dodo bird was a success just so far as it helped the species reproduce; apparently the Dodo existed on Earth for a long time before it was exterminated in the nineteenth century.

What we should say, then, is that up to the present, human intelligence has shown itself to be a successful evolutionary adaptation. But in regard to our intelligence *that is all the theory of evolution implies*. It is crucial to notice that evolutionary success is not the same thing as

9. If we suppose that an alien race supervised our evolution, it hardly solves the problem. How did *that* species evolve to have truth-focused intelligence?

10. The one possible exception is social evolution among advanced social species (i.e. human beings and maybe, to a tiny degree, some apes, but not bees or ants). Human cultural achievements, such as speech and writing, are passed down socially, not genetically, and yet these achievements enhance our reproductive fitness. But human cultural achievements depend on human intelligence, and intelligence is passed on genetically. Genetically speaking, human intellectual capacities have not changed in the last 20,000 years; all our cultural achievements have been wrought with Stone Age brains.

success in discovering truth, what philosophers would call "epistemic success."

All our scientific theories have been produced by the use of human intelligence. Evolution implies that human intelligence is a good tool for reproducing our genes (at least, it has been 'til now). Nothing in evolution implies that human intelligence is a good tool for *gaining truth* unless knowing truth somehow gives us an advantage in passing on our genes.

Of course, knowing some truths does confer a reproductive advantage. Recognizing tigers and tornados is a great advantage if I can also think of ways to protect my children from them. But how does recognizing abstract truths help me pass on my genes? For instance, how does recognizing the truth of evolution help a species succeed?

Here is way to press the point a bit further. The vast majority of human beings, both in the past and today, believe in God, the "gods," or some other religious doctrine. According to modern naturalism, all these beliefs are false, and this creates a minor problem for modern naturalism. Why is it that so many people believe in God when in fact there is no God? For the modern naturalist, this is a scientific question, a question to be answered by evolutionary psychology. And the evolutionary psychologists have proposed possible answers: religious beliefs are widespread among human beings because such beliefs (more precisely, the intellectual capacities that underlie such beliefs) promote reproductive success. Do you see the result? Religious beliefs are not true, but nevertheless human beings have evolved in such a way that many of us are predisposed to believe them.

According to evolution, the same thing may well be true of other beliefs. Those beliefs may not be true, but we have evolved in such a way that many of us are predisposed to believe them. This leads to an odd and interesting result: if evolution is true, then we may well be wrong about our abstract theories, including evolution.

The philosopher Alvin Plantinga (from whom we borrowed this fifth argument) makes this observation. If we believe in a God who could direct evolution according to a plan, then we could have confidence that our evolved intellectual capacities would be directed at truth, not just reproduction. The theory of evolution, when combined with belief in a Creator, does not undermine confidence in our abstract theories. But evolution combined with modern naturalism does.

Why should we think modern naturalism is true when it undermines our confidence that our intellectual capacities are good tools for finding truth?

CONCLUSION

Remember, we do not claim that these reasons for suspicion "prove" that modern naturalism is false. We are only planting seeds of suspicion. For many people in the world today, the modern naturalistic worldview is taken for granted. If you consider the reasons we have listed in this chapter—and we only presented five out of many possible reasons—we think you may be dissatisfied with the naturalist's worldview. At the least, you will question it. You may discover that you live in a world of great mystery.

4

How to Think About Religion

Synopsis: The world's religions take mystery seriously, an advantage over modern naturalism. In this chapter we describe three ways to think about the relationship between the religions, and we say why we prefer inclusivism to pluralism or exclusivism.

I N THE NOVEL *THE Life of Pi*,[1] the main character, a teenage boy named Pi, finds himself practicing Christianity, Islam and Hinduism—at the same time! He attends church, mosque and the Hindu temple. One day, he and his family are out together when the Hindu pandit, the Christian priest, and the Muslim imam all converge on the teenage boy and his family. Each one seems intent on praising Pi's religiosity but only when that religiosity is limited to his own religion. The result of this happenstance meeting of religious leaders isn't pretty. Each leader is fighting for the truth of his own religion, and the boy's parents are very upset. How could Pi even think of being a Christian, a Muslim and a Hindu—at the same time?!? The boy, however, has a challenging time understanding why he shouldn't pursue all the paths available to him. He reports that he's only trying to love God. Pi makes for an interesting case study. We point him out as a way of introducing the subject of this chapter, namely, how should a person think about the diversity of religions found in our world?

Life, we think, is full of mystery. In the previous chapter, we argued that the natural order points toward mystery. Why is there something rather than nothing? Why does the natural order provide for the pos-

---

1. Martel, *Pi.*

sibility of life? Even mathematics seems, in some ways, very mysterious. Let's be careful, though. Thus far we have only *pointed* toward mystery and extended an invitation. We have not argued for anything more than that we should be open to mystery. In fact, our argument has been largely negative, consisting mainly of the claim that modern naturalism chokes off the sense of mystery that nature itself seems to contain. We do not plan to explore nature any further in this book. Rather we want to consider what we think is an area of human experience where mystery is most directly dealt with: religion. Yet we think something else important needs to be done before we talk about how various religions handle human mystery. That step is to consider what a person's basic attitude toward the various religions should be. In order to do that, we need to make some observations and important distinctions. We'll then tell you which view we take on the matter.

AN ANALYSIS INTRODUCED BY AN ANALOGY

One way to proceed is by an analogy. Suppose there were two quite different medical philosophies. Both philosophies hold that the result of good medical care is good health. These two philosophies, however, make different assumptions, which imply different understandings of what good health is. One—call it the holistic approach—says a person should exercise daily, eat the right foods, avoid human-made medications, and practice sound mind/body meditation. A person following these rules, it is thought, will have good health, which means that the general state of one's body will be optimum. That is, the state of one's body will be positive—in fact, as positive as is possible—and because of this, one will be able to fight off diseases of all types. The other medical philosophy—call it the technical view—says one should avail oneself of whatever technological and surgical advances humans can discover or invent. One will thereby have good health, which means that one will avoid dying because of one or another illness. There is, thus, no "optimum" on this view. Rather, this view is based on the notion of curing problems when they set in—a defensive approach. The holistic model, in contrast, is an offensive approach—don't let the problems set in to begin with.

Now both these philosophies prescribe a set of beliefs about how to live one's life and about the results of living that way. Both capture the results by the phrase "good health." Let's call the former of each pair (the "how to live life" part) the "means" and the latter of each pair (the "what effect it has" part) the "end" and the overall result (good health) "the ultimate goal."

A little thought will show how aspects of these two medical philosophies can (and probably do) overlap in real life. After all, the goal of good medical care is good health, including both taking the offense to optimize the overall state of good health *and* a defensive view—avoiding death at the hands of some disease or other. But let's suppose, for the sake of the illustration, that there are several views on how these two philosophies work together. One we can call "pluralist," which says that both philosophies are true and not ultimately conflicting. This is probably what most of us think about the holistic and the technical approaches in general. But you will notice that there is one fairly obvious conflict. The holistic claim that we should avoid human-made medications conflicts more or less directly with the technical claim that we should avail ourselves of whatever human advances we have at our disposal. The holistic and the technical do not go so easily together. It would, in short, be difficult to say they are both literally true. So the pluralist might do a couple of different things. She might first say that both are "true" but in some way "fictional" (perhaps in the way that a metaphor can be both "true" and "fictional") so that there is no real conflict between the two. The important point is that we reach the ultimate goal (good health) rather than the details of the means and ends. In short, there is no actual reality to either means or ends (both are illusory), but the ultimate goal is, of course, not illusory. The pluralist might like to say that the ultimate goal is obvious, but it's hard to agree, since both the means and the ends of both medical philosophies are "fictional." This pluralist approach to medical philosophies is probably the hardest to grasp, since with medicine we are working at least in part with empirical, measurable methods and ends. It is hard to know what the pluralist might mean by a "fictional" understanding of eating good food or undergoing surgery. But for now, let's just overlook these difficulties.

The second pluralistic take is more graspable. This pluralist might simply claim that both philosophies are true (not fictional) and that any given person can reach the "end" of each philosophy, even though the means and ends conflict and no single person could hold both. One person eats wisely, exercises, meditates, never sees a doctor and achieves optimal health. The other person visits physicians whenever threatened by disease and thus avoids death. According to this second kind of pluralism, each person has achieved "good health" (the ultimate goal). Notice that if this approach to pluralism is taken, the end shapes the ultimate goal. In other words, on this view there are plural accounts of the ultimate goal, good health.

A completely different response to our "medical philosophies" question is what we can call exclusivism. This view says that at best only one of these philosophies is true, although it is possible that neither one is true. Here it is worth noting that there is a difference between a strict contradiction (A and ~A cannot both be true at the same time) and what philosophers call contraries (A and B cannot both be true, although both could be false and C true instead). There are a number of obvious ways in which neither could be true. The means of each could be false. The ends of each could be false. Or there might not actually be an ultimate goal.[2] If there is no ultimate goal, of course, no matter what the ends are (of these or any other medical philosophy), no medical philosophy claiming that good health is possible will be true. Let's set that issue aside and assume there is an ultimate goal. If so, each philosophy could fail because its ends or its means fail to describe reality. But we know that if the holistic philosophy is true, the technical is false, and if the technical is true, the holistic is false. Hence, the term "exclusive."

More needs to be said here. Let's distinguish between the *overall* description of the medical philosophy (what it actually claims to be true in total) and *partial* descriptions of the view. Here we can see that, taken piecemeal, the two views need not conflict at every point. For example, in a broad sense, they don't conflict on the ultimate goal. But they do conflict on the particulars of the goal—what we've called "the end." One says its goal is to optimize one's bodily condition—the offensive position. The other says its goal is to avoid dying—the defensive position. Perhaps one might be able to argue that these two are not, strictly, conflicting. After all, if one dies, one's body is not in optimum condition! Perhaps the ends don't actually conflict. But when it comes to means, the holistic and the technical philosophies clearly do conflict, as we noted above.

2. Here the reader might note that goals are rather funny because one can have as a goal something that doesn't exist. You can, for example, run in order to become healthy but never become healthy. What we mean by there being no ultimate goal is that, in some cases, the goal is a false one, impossible to obtain because there simply is no such thing. For instance, achieving good health might be like having the goal of making gold from lead—you can try if you want, but lead-based gold is a chemical impossibility.

Completely avoiding human-made medications is not compatible with using the latest medical developments in surgery or medication. The exclusivist analysis of medical philosophies will say that, to the degree that the partial descriptions conflict, the two overall philosophies must conflict, and to that extent at least one must be wrong. If partial descriptions can conflict, then the overall descriptions conflict.[3] Such conflicting claims ought not to be held (at the same time) by a thoughtful person. Note also that on exclusivism, one can't get around conflicts by claiming that the descriptions are somehow fictional. That would likely end us in some sort of pluralism.[4]

A third possibility is what we'll call inclusivism. On this view, only one of the philosophies can actually be correct as well, but believers in the other philosophy can still reach the ultimate goal. Here the ultimate goal is reached (along with the end) via the truth of the actually correct philosophy. Let's say the holistic medical approach is the correct one. According to inclusivism, the ultimate goal of good health can be reached by either philosophy *but only because the holistic approach is true.* How does this work? Well, suppose, for example, that one was fortunate enough to be born with an overall healthy body to begin with and that one prefers the foods of the holistic diet and happens to like the relaxing feeling of mind/body meditation and happens never to take any human-made medication. However, one's beliefs are all messed up. You might still believe the technical model and would be more than willing to go "under the knife" or to take whatever pills your MD prescribes for you. Your faith, so to speak, is in the wrong place, but the reality of the situation makes you healthy. The point is, those who hold to the holistic view have the correct view, and you just happen to get the benefit of it *even though you don't believe the correct things.* Here you can see that even though your overall beliefs are faulty, you are still living life the right way and that fact is what brings you to good health. If you didn't do something right, then it would be difficult to see how the ultimate goal could be reached.

3. This follows a basic rule of logic that says in order for "A and B" to be true, "A" and "B" must be true separately. So if either "A" or "B" (partial descriptions) are false, than "A and B" (the overall description) is false as well.

4. Mark thinks that fictional truths can conflict with one another, but that is a deep and difficult subject best left for more advanced discussions.

A slightly more technical way to state the inclusivist view is that what brings about the ultimate goal is the ontology of the situation. "Ontology" is just a philosophy word for "the way things are." On the example given here, the way things are is that the holistic model is true and, because of that, our technical believer obtains good health, even though the technical believer is wrong in her actual beliefs.

THE ANALYSIS APPLIED TO RELIGION

Let's return to *The Life of Pi*, whose protagonist practices three different religions and whose religious teachers and parents are quite upset to discover this fact about young Pi. Of course, on the modern naturalist's model of reality, the conflicting claims of world religions in describing reality should be ignored. After all, any religious experiences in which they might be based are reducible to physical states of the brain. If we take them literally, all religious claims are false, because they point to a reality outside the neurophysiological structures to which evolution brought us. But the authors don't accept the reductionism of naturalism. We think it closes off mystery. Here it is worth noting that we believe naturalism doesn't just close off religious mystery. It closes off *all* mystery. Not only does religion exit the stage, but so do beauty, truth, and goodness. In fact, these things don't merely exit the stage; rather, they leave the modern naturalist theatre altogether. Yet we aren't willing to think the world devoid of meaning. And neither, apparently, is Pi. He loves the mystery of life and wants to embrace multiple religious approaches to mystery and meaning. Like Pi, we think that if the door is open to non-natural meaning, then it should be open to religious meaning. We hope you, by this point in the book, are open to meaning of all sorts as well, including religious meaning. If so, congratulations on having reached this far on the journey toward mystery! There are a lot of more or less "weird" things that need explaining. Why is there something rather than nothing? How is it possible that human minds can explore the real universe? And so on.

Religious ways of explanation are one way to explore and understand the mysteries of the universe. Religious belief has a long-standing history of explaining mystery—far longer than what we think of as science. But religious belief is not without problems. One challenge to religious belief is that there seem to be too many ways of believing or living one's religious life. Pi's response is to follow three of the major religions at the same time. If we don't think Pi's response to the problem is the best one (and we don't), then how should we understand the competing religious claims of so many people?

We want to take some of the notions developed in the medical philosophy analogy and apply them in the context of religion. Recall the difference between the means, the end and the ultimate goal. In the context of our discussion of religion, the ultimate goal is salvation, whereas the ends are different—for example, heaven for Christians, nirvana for Buddhists, moksha for Hindus and so forth. These ends are not described in the same way (even though there may be some overlaps in some cases). Nor are the means described in the same way. In Christianity one needs an appropriate relationship with God in Jesus Christ. In Buddhism, living meditatively is important, and in Hinduism, the life of learning and scholarship or a life following a guru can be good paths (among others). It will also help to recall the distinction between overall and partial descriptions. A partial description of Christianity (let's say, that God created the world) overlaps with certain branches of Hinduism and more clearly with Islam and Judaism. Nevertheless, the overall descriptions of these religions do not agree. Judaism may or may not include the notion of heaven, and neither Judaism nor Islam has a Trinitarian notion of God, which Christianity does.

The young protagonist in *The Life of Pi* expresses well some sort of pluralism. There are many versions of religious pluralism, but the basic idea is that all the religions are true, in their own right. Whether one is a Buddhist, a Jew, or a Jain, one's basic religious beliefs are true. Of course, what is meant by "true," when the claims of the various religions (taken at face value) deeply conflict with each other, is a bit of a challenge. For example, if Christianity is true, there is an afterlife in which one can live forever happily in the presence of God, a kind of ultimate flourishing. If certain versions of Buddhism are true, then there is no afterlife for an individual person (in part, because there are, in the end, no actual individual persons). One way to handle such conflicts is to suggest that, if a given person believes in a Christian heaven, she ends up there, but if she lives a Buddhist life, "she" ends up, as the Buddhists claim, in an Enlightened state (nirvana). Another way to handle the conflicting claims is the suggestion that none of the religious claims is literally true but point (in complicated ways suggested by some philosophers and theologians) to a reality that none of the religious descriptions can, in this life, accurately describe.[5] These two approaches to religious pluralism parallel the pluralisms described above when we talked about medical philosophies. It is easier to see, however, how one can think of the means/ends components of religious life as fictional than it is to understand the empirically oriented and measurable claims of medicine as fictional. This is one place the analogy might break down. But we are using the analogy as an illustration, not as an argument, so we hope this is not a big problem.

Other pluralistic possibilities exist as well, but we won't go into details. The main point is that, on a pluralistic view, all the religious positions are true, or at least they accurately describe a path to understanding/explaining mystery or ultimate reality. Pluralism is quite popular today. It is tempting to think pluralism is a result of postmodernism, but that isn't accurate. Pluralism is found in the ancient Western philosophical world and, in fact, among the religions themselves, a point we'll return to below. Its roots are far deeper than postmodernism.

A second way of understanding the conflicting religious truth claims is exclusivism. On one level, exclusivism says, basically, that whenever two religious truth claims conflict, only one (at best) can accurately describe the situation. This relies on the notion that any falsity of a partial description entails that the overall description is false as well. So, if any significant part of the religious description is false, the overall description is as well. Thus, if Judaism claims there is a God and (some version of) Hinduism claims there is no God at all, at best only one of these claims can be true. Hence, only one of these overall religions can be true. Of course, there can be lots of true partial descriptions and these can overlap across religions. For example, all the great religions claim that one should act morally (there are many versions of the golden rule), and most claim that there is something real beyond the physical universe.

Here we want to note that of course one might get some less important aspect of reality wrong on a given religious view and the view still be *basically* correct. Even within a given religion there are some pretty substantial differences. Consider the differences among Orthodox, Roman Catholic and the myriad of Protestant Christian believers. All have Jesus at the center of their accounts of Christianity, but some believe in purgatory and others do not. Some hold Mary in quite high esteem; others do

5. Hick, *Religion*.

not. So for the most part, we want to talk in broad generalities about the basic framework of a religion rather than its debatable details—details debatable even within the religious traditions themselves. The distinction between basic and debatable is perhaps a hard distinction to make, but to give a rough idea, it is a basic difference among religions that some are theistic (hold to an all-knowing, all-powerful, all-good God who created the world) and some are nontheistic (such as certain branches of Hinduism). Another example is that some religions affirm that God incarnated the divine being into the world (Christianity, some branches of Hinduism) while others do not (Judaism or Islam). Again, this distinction is hard to make out except in very broad outline. Fortunately, we don't have to make out the details for our discussion here. Nevertheless, the distinction is important and we hope the general idea is clear. A religion may be basically correct but wrong on some detail or other.

Exclusivism goes on to say that whichever religion captures the basic truths about the right religious path is the true one. This would include, of course, the means, the end, and the ultimate goal, that is, how to live and believe, the result of such living and believing, and, of course, what we are calling "salvation." On exclusivism, the ultimate goal cannot, in fact, be separated from the end (they would, in fact, be exactly the same). In some ways, exclusivism is messier than pluralism is, for not all the major world religions claim to be exclusive about their beliefs. For example, certain versions of Hinduism are themselves pluralistic. Perhaps a personal illustration might help here. Years ago, Mark invited a good friend of his (his nick-name is Bappa) over for a visit. It happened to be a few days after Christmas. Bappa, a self-described "cultural Hindu," asked Mark, "What did you do on Christmas?" to which Mark replied, "Well, we opened presents, had a nice meal. What did you do?" (Notice Mark hadn't gone to church to worship the new-born King of the universe as perhaps one might think a good Christian should!) Bappa replied, "I went down to the (historic) Christian mission and meditated," and then he smiled his winning smile. Bappa was making the point that some Hindus believe all religious paths ultimately lead to moksha (the Hindu salvation), and Bappa was, tongue in cheek, laughing about the fact that he had taken the Christian holy day more seriously than the Christian!

However, Mark later returned the jest. One day he noted to Bappa, "If Hinduism is true, then I, as a Christian, will obtain moksha (the

Hindu salvation), right?" "Yes," said Bappa. "But then," replied Mark, "If Christianity is true, and you don't accept Jesus, then you are in deep trouble, right?" There was lots of laughter. Bappa and Mark continued the dialogue about Hinduism and Christianity until they both moved to different universities. Christianity and Islam (and perhaps some other religions as well) seem, at face value, to be exclusivist, while others are not. Some people think, however, that all religions, in their basic descriptions of ultimate reality, are forced, by logic, to be exclusivist in at least some of their claims.

Here we want to separate two issues. First is the issue of accurate description. What we mean here is that at the basic level—at a sort of core description—of a religion, the description is either true or false. Now, getting the core description of a religion may be more complicated than at first appears, for religions are complex social and cultural webs of belief, activity, and ritual. But we think that, once one gets to the core description, there will be more or less explicit conflicts of descriptions across religions. It is, for example, built into Christianity that the final story of the world includes a real God who created the world and who came as a human person (Jesus) to live among human persons. We killed Jesus but he rose from the dead. This description is meant to be an actual description of the world. It is not, in short, meant to be a fiction even though some folks take it that way (including some Christians). The vast majority of Christians just take it to be true. On the other hand, on at least one version of Hinduism (advaita Vedanta), there is no God (as Western people typically understand God) but rather only a non-duality. In the famous saying, Atman (the individual human person) and Brahman (ultimate reality) are one. The world is an illusion. Now on such a view, even Christianity is an illusion. In one sense, then, there is no conflict between the two core descriptions, for the Christian description turns out, if advaita Vedanta is correct, to be illusory. However, on another level, the two do conflict, for Christianity assumes that it is not an illusion, in which case one of the core teachings of advaita Vedanta is false. The main point is that in some way, the core descriptions of religions, even those that are pluralistic in some manner (as advaita Vedanta is in terms of how one can reach moksha), are in conflict.

The second issue is not description but what we are going to call the "salvation question." Here we want to talk about how one must live the right life (and hence, believe the right things)—"the means"—in virtue of which one is "saved." We remind the reader that we are using the term "saved" very broadly so that not only the Christian heaven but the Buddhist nirvana and the Hindu moksha and so forth all count as "salvation." Now the question is, how does one get saved? One can be an exclusivist here, believing that there is only one right path to salvation to the exclusion of all others. Remember, not all religions are exclusive when it comes to the salvation question. Certain versions of Hinduism are not exclusive, whereas certain versions of Christianity and Islam are clearly exclusive. But here there are more questions, for even if the paths to salvation are many for a Hindu, the ultimate nature of that salvation may not be. Probably few Hindus would believe that a Christian ends up in a Christian heaven. Perhaps good Christians will end up reincarnated in a better form here on Earth in the next life or perhaps simply reach moksha (and hence be free of the wheel of reincarnation) directly. But moksha is freedom from illusion and not a Christian-like heaven.

So the connections between accurate description and salvation in fact are quite complex. One version of pluralism says that all religious descriptions are descriptively true and that each religious path leads to its own version of salvation. Another version says that none of the descriptions are literally true but there is a salvation (of the same sort) for all religious people (and perhaps all people) after this life (or perhaps after many reincarnated lives).

Exclusivism is no less complicated, for one can be exclusive about description and salvation (sometimes having the right description leads necessarily to salvation—as seems true in some versions of Christianity) or perhaps about one and not the other (one can be a descriptive exclusivist as a Hindu and hence a pluralist about salvation). Suppose you hold to both descriptive and to salvation exclusivism, in which case you think that one's religious path is both true and the only way to salvation. In this case, if you happen to be wrong about the religious description of the means, then you will lose your salvation. In fact, you never had it, since the description is faulty. But would you lose the ultimate goal of salvation? Perhaps not if some other more pluralistic religion is true. (A devout Muslim and a devout Jew might both be wrong about what the proper end of religion is, but each might still achieve moksha—assuming that Hinduism's view of ultimate salvation is correct.) In contrast, one might be a salvation exclusivist (the nature of salvation is fixed but how you get there—the rest of the description—is not). Such a person believes there are many true paths to get to salvation. But thinking about this a little will lead you to note that this is just a version of pluralism.

This brings us to the third possible way of thinking about the various religions. It's called inclusivism, again in a manner analogous to the inclusivism of the medical philosophies. On this model, there is only one true description (on basics at least, and perhaps right down to the very details), and yet because of the nature of the religion, others outside the religion might receive salvation even though they don't have the right means. This is a little tricky, however, for what should be included in the notion of the "means?" Is it the way one lives or the beliefs one has? If you remember the medical analogy above, the person reaches good health not because of her or his beliefs but because of the way the person lives. She happens to eat right, avoid human-made medications, and meditates but she doesn't believe those things provide good health. The point is that on the analogy, the person has to do something right to be "saved." It is more complicated with religion, however, for it is not always clear what it means to "live right." Living well or rightly often includes beliefs. In fact, one could argue that what one does really shows what one actually believes. Even with this complication, however, the important point is that what saves you in the context of an inclusivist understanding of religion is the actual reality of the religion, that is, the fact that a given religion is true. There is a terrific illustration of this view in C.S. Lewis's *The Chronicles of Narnia*. Near the end of *The Last Battle*, Emeth, a faithful follower of Tash, the false god, accepts a challenge and expresses his longing to look on the face of Tash. Later, having taken the challenge, he discovers not Tash but Aslan, the real God in the story. It was the faithfulness, honesty and commitment of Emeth that leads him, in the end, to the real means of salvation.[6]

There is a further issue, perhaps a little more technical but very helpful. When a person refers to something, she can refer by using the wrong terms. Suppose I say to you, "Mary is that person over there, holding the soda in her hand." Now I've referred to Mary. You can pick Mary out now. Suppose, however, she wasn't holding soda but a glass of water. Did I refer to Mary or not? Yes, even though part of the description was wrong. Another example. Suppose I tell you to cut down the maple tree in the front yard. But suppose I wouldn't know a maple tree from a Douglas fir and neither do you. Nevertheless, you go and cut down the

6. See Lewis, *Last Battle*, 185–88.

only tree in the front yard. Obviously, I've referred to the right tree and you've gotten the reference because you end up cutting down the right tree. The point is this: we can refer to something well enough, even if our descriptions are largely inaccurate.

So let's keep these two things in mind; first, the connection between living one's life and what one really believes and the possibility of reference even though the description is faulty. Let us then illustrate how inclusivism might work in the case of our own religious commitments, namely, Christianity. Suppose Christianity is true, both in means and in the end. To keep it brief, the appropriate relationship with Jesus is the means (which rests on what we might call the "underlying means," namely, the work of Jesus on the cross and in the resurrection), and the end is life forever in the presence of the Triune-Creator God. On Christian grounds, the end is identical to the ultimate goal. But the means is limited to the right relationship with Jesus. How, then, can someone who is not explicitly a Christ-follower be saved? In part the answer lies in the nature of God. God loves everyone so much that the divine love provides the underlying means of salvation to all (the work of the incarnate Jesus in the cross and his resurrection). Of course, we humans must respond to this by developing an appropriate relationship with Jesus. A person could develop such a relationship explicitly, by committing oneself to be a follower of Jesus, by a life of prayer and learning to will what Jesus wills, by loving one's neighbors, and so on. Or, a relationship with Jesus might develop implicitly. A committed Hindu who lives a faithful Hindu life according to one of the possible paths for a Hindu might illustrate the latter case. Now it is entirely possible that he makes references to various gods and goddesses of the Hindu pantheon (or alternately, uses the nondualistic language of advaita Vedanta and speaks of Brahman as the ultimate, nontheistic reality) but all the while is referring to Jesus. This person lives out a very moral life, loving his neighbor. He will, in short, flourish. In *The Last Battle*, Aslan tells Emeth he will count all of Emeth's devotion to Tash as devotion to Aslan; it seems that Emeth thought he was worshiping Tash when he actually was worshiping Aslan.

Some Christians will not agree with this interpretation of Christianity and insist that one must not just live a good life but explicitly believe in Jesus. This raises the question about the relationship between how one lives and what one actually believes. If asked about what he believes, the Hindu will not say he believes that Jesus is the only way to salvation. From within the Christian camp, such a reply will show (it is thought by many Christians) that our Hindu believer is not a Christian! Since only Christians, it is thought, go to heaven, this person is not going to heaven, that is, is not saved. After all, the apostle Peter, when hauled before the Sanhedrin for preaching the gospel, said: "Salvation is found in no one else, for there is no other name under heaven given to people by which we much be saved" (Acts 4:12).

Our reply has two parts. First, it seems that the Bible contains stories of people who received God's grace even though they did not believe correctly or fully. It can be argued that this is precisely what Paul teaches about Abraham in Galatians. In Galatians, Paul is eager to defend his doctrine of salvation by faith, not by works, against those who say Christians have to obey Jewish law. To make his case, Paul points out that the greatest hero of the Torah, Abraham, was saved by faith, not by keeping the law (Galatians 3:6-18). Abraham *believed* the promise, Paul emphasizes. But then Paul goes on to make a seemingly strange point: the promise was about Abraham's "seed," not "seeds"—one, not many. Paul says this means the promise was about Jesus. The upshot of this is that Paul teaches that Abraham was *saved by faith in Jesus*. In point of fact, Abraham knew little about Jesus except God's promise. Our inclusivist position holds that people today can be saved by faith in Jesus even though they know almost nothing about Jesus.

Our second point is this. We believe deeply that Jesus taught us not to judge the eternal end of other people. We just don't know who will be in heaven and who won't be. So, judging a person's eternal state is something best left up to God. All we are suggesting is one way to think about the relationship between Christianity and the other religions. It is the way *we* think about the world religions and Christianity. The reader need not agree, but we invite you to think about it.

To return to the relationship between how one believes and how one lives, we think how one lives speaks more loudly than what one says. If all the fruits of the Christian spiritual life are present in someone who says she believes something different, we think that although her description is false, what she refers to is correct. The relationship between reference and belief is a very complex philosophical issue but we hope we've said enough for our readers to get the basic point. We simply want to note our openness to what one actually believes being expressed, finally, in what one does. Integrity seems to demand that much, and we want to leave open the details of how that all might go.

There are several other important things to observe. First, the view we are suggesting does not entail that everyone will be saved. On our view, it is possible for someone to reject God's offer of salvation in Jesus (whether he knows much or little about Jesus). Second, our view does not entail that all the religions are true. We have explicitly said that salvation comes to human beings through the God-Human, Jesus. Religions that deny this are, at least in that respect, false. Third, our view does not mean that the Buddhist or Hindu path is an acceptable means to salvation. Given the truth of Christianity, the means to salvation is an appropriate relationship with Jesus. It is possible, we think, for a Buddhist or Hindu to have such a relationship with Jesus even under an inaccurate description of Jesus. Fourth, on our view, some religious paths may be closer than others to the truth. Judaism, for example, being theistic, is closer to an accurate description of the salvific path than is Buddhism. Yet in the end, it is the life and work of Jesus, the divine Son of God, which provides the actual means to the ultimate goal.

Our view does not entail that there are no good reasons to become a Christian if one is a Buddhist or Muslim or something else. If Christianity is true, one gets a fuller picture of salvation reality within Christianity. In fact, we think there are good reasons to think Christianity is a fuller, more complete account of the world than the other religions. In the next chapter, we will give some reasons why we think aspects of the alternative religions are further from the truth than Christianity.

In sum, inclusivism is exclusivist about its description (of the means, the end, and the ultimate goal) but not exclusivist about salvation itself. A person can be saved because of the truth of Christianity without necessarily following the means, *as the typical Christian might understand them.* Here we could get into all kinds of discussion about the details of the means of salvation according to Christianity. As Christians, we think it clear that no human is, in the end, to judge the final state before God of any other person. We take that as our starting point.

That leaves us with lots of room to discuss and learn from people of other faiths. It even leaves us room to discuss whether other religions are true or at least partially true. It does not take away a basic thrust of the Christian faith, namely, that the good news of Jesus' life, death, and resurrection should be shared with everyone. It may (and we presume does) lead to the salvation of many people. Perhaps hearing the gospel (which is just another word for "good news") helps people take their own lives more seriously and thus sets them on the path of salvation. For others, perhaps the sharing of the gospel is not a means of salvation but the opening for developing a better, more accurate description of the world.

We said earlier that one can approach apologetics with the notion of "knock down" arguments for Christianity. We said, too, that we don't want to knock down anyone, including people whose faith is different than is ours. It is time now to open the door to a dialogue with other religions and to think about the actual beliefs and practices of various religions.

5

How the Religions Address Mystery

Synopsis: The major religions of the world take mystery seriously (an advantage over modern naturalism). As inclusivists, we have said that followers of the religions may have a saving relationship with Jesus, perhaps without knowing it. In this chapter we give a very brief description of several important religions. In each case, we point to what we think are good features of the religion, but we also explain why we think Christianity is better.

IN OUR CULTURE, WHEN we compare the great challenges and difficulty of the natural sciences—physics, chemistry, biology—to religious subjects, the latter are often thought of as rather mushy and easy. In fact, anyone who has studied various religions in any detail knows that religion and the philosophical notions that attend to the religions are very complex and sometimes quite difficult to understand. Still, the sciences are often held up as the "objective, cold, hard" subjects, subjects that will lead us to Truth (with a capital T). The subjects covered by the humanities, in contrast, are often thought of as subjective, warm, and soft. The human sciences, psychology, anthropology, sociology, and economics, are thought of as somewhere in between in rigor and substance since they are somewhere between the natural sciences and humanities in content.

Perhaps many in this culture think this because the supposed difficulty of a subject is thought to be tied to the so-called "objectivity" of the subject. We, however, reject this understanding of the nature of the sciences and the humanities. The "cold, hard objective" nature of the natural sciences is, we think, rooted in a nineteenth century notion of physics. As we argued earlier, physics is not observer-neutral. In fact, the very nature of the quantum world seems affected by our interaction with it. The comforting, fixed objectivity of the nineteenth century version of physics simply doesn't exist. Since we reject the notion of a totalizing objectivity and also reject the reducibility of freedom, consciousness, and other mysterious things to physics, we reject the notion that the sciences are more objective, cold, or hard than the humanities. Stated another way, we reject the notion that the humanities are more subjective, warm, or soft than the natural sciences. In some ways, the humanities, dealing as they do with human nature, are perhaps more difficult (hence the challenges of finding agreement) than the natural sciences.

The reason we are spending some time on this point at the beginning of a chapter on the mystery of religion is that we want to emphasize how important we think religious questions are, and that we both believe deeply in answers to these questions. Having admitted those two points, however, we want to emphasize further that because of the difficulty of these questions, the best sorts of answers a person can give are always embedded in the context in which one lives. Our understanding of what it is to be a person is framed in significant ways by our local communities and our larger cultures. Thus, to answer the question "what is a person?" independent of those communities and cultures would be to give the humanities a role that the natural sciences were thought to have in the nineteenth century. Such an approach gives too much weight to objectivity and not enough to subjectivity. We prefer something like "inter-subjectivity" as a term to describe the human adventure of tracking down the mysteries of the human person and, for that matter, the natural world as well.

Having covered some preliminaries, we now state the goals of this chapter. The first goal is to describe some of the major world religions. The best we hope to do in this regard are simple sketches of religious beliefs—the very barest outlines of our sense of various major world religions. In the next chapter, we will explain why we are Christians with this discussion of the religions as background. We admit ahead of time that we cannot do justice to the various religions. There are many more than we can cover well in a short space and we cannot come anywhere near covering all the different aspects or schools or patterns of thought within each religion. Just as in chapter 3 where we gave a brief description of modern naturalism and counted on our readers to fill in details, here we provide only a sketch of each religion we discuss (and we won't even mention some religions).

Our second goal is to say briefly what we think is right about the various religions and what we think is not so accurate. What we have to say is shaped by who we are as persons. We are Westerners. We are also Christians who happen to be of a Protestant flavor. One of us is a Quaker and the other an Anglican. Finally, we both take the Bible seriously. That is, we do not believe the Bible can or should be in its entirety "de-mythologized." We think parts of it describe important historical events, while other parts are poetic, parabolic, theological, etc. Some of those historical events (such as the death and resurrection of Jesus) have significant theological and salvation importance. We are both inclusivists about the gospel, as we discussed in the previous chapter. So our responses to the religions are meant as points of dialogue and learning rather than an attempt at knockdown criticisms of religions other than our own. In fact, we both can be critical of certain aspects of our own religion and various cultural expressions of it.

We think that the best we can do as people reflecting about these matters is to think within our situations. It is impossible for human beings to give a completely neutral, objective description of religious beliefs. But to state it that way is far too negative. We think, in fact, that being culturally and historically situated is exactly the way God made humans to be and that we should celebrate our circumstance. This aspect of being human is postmodern, no matter how disappointing it may seem from the nineteenth-century eyes we inherited, or perhaps to people trained to think of their religious commitments as involving some sort of Cartesian-like certainty.

There are a variety of ways in which scholars discuss the religions of the world. One can take a sociological approach, a historical approach, a theological or philosophical approach, and so on. The approach we'll take is largely theological and philosophical or, more broadly, a worldview approach, although we cannot avoid some historical comments. We will try to capture some of the main ways in which a person living in the world of a given religion might think about various philosophical or theological matters. We will thus be rather anachronistic and certainly not exhaustive. First we will discuss the nontheistic religions (or versions of the various religions that are nontheistic) and then the more generally theistic ones. Other organizational themes will become apparent as we move through the discussion. Please note too that we will not discuss Native American religion, traditional African religion, Shinto, Taoism or the great expressions of Buddhism found outside its roots in India. This has more to do with space than anything else.

INDIAN ANTECEDENTS

We will begin with the three great Indian religions: Jainism, Buddhism, and Hinduism. These three major religions have their roots in the ancient religion of India, often referred to as Vedic religion. We won't cover details of the Vedic religion except to note a couple of points that helped bring about the development of the other three major Eastern religions we'll discuss. First, Vedic religion was polytheistic but with a twist: something called "kathenotheism" or "one-god-at-a-time-ism." This plays an important role in the rest of the history of the Indian religions. Second, the gods were generally thought to come into existence with creation (or to have existed along with the world, which may or may not have been created in time). Also in Vedic religion there were hints of the notion of the more or less constant death and rebirth of humans, a fact that is interpreted differently by each of the three major Indian religions.

JAINISM

Jainism is a very old religion rooted in ancient India. Although in very early Vedic religion there were many gods, Jainism is fundamentally atheistic. Or at least if there are gods, humans have no particular need of them. Jainism is, arguably, one of the most conservative of all the religions, as it is known for its consistency of thought. For example, there are very few divisions among Jains on basic beliefs. The one major division is that between the "Sky-clad" and the "White-clad" among the monks, which has to do with whether the commitment to total austerity requires the monk to be naked (Sky-clad) or it permits him to wear clothes (White-clad). Doctrinally, the Jains are very consistent, compared to other religions.

One of the key thoughts is the notion of Fordmakers. The universe is eternal (there being no creator God), and Fordmakers are teachers who enable the faithful to cross the stream of existence to reach the other side. Fordmakers are human but transcend the gods. There are many Fordmakers, the most recent of which are Parsva and Mahavira. Before his birth, Parsva was living in heaven (part of the Jain cosmos) as the god Indra. After being born as a human, he eventually withdrew to the forest and, through the practice of austerity and yoga, he obtained omniscience and assurance of liberation from this world. He then taught others his message. Mahavira was the son of two pious Jains. He, too, withdrew from the world and through austerity obtained motionless, changeless existence and became a teacher.

Two important themes emerge from the lives of the later Fordmakers, omniscience (and hence release from this world) and the doctrine of karma. Generally in Eastern religions, the human problem is not sin as much as it is spiritual ignorance. In Jainism, the doctrine of omniscience provides a means of overcoming spiritual ignorance, so omniscience is not mere theoretical knowledge but practical and experiential knowledge of how to live appropriately in terms of spirit. Jains believe that everyone is, in principle, capable of omniscience. Once having attained such knowledge, one can be freed from karma. "Karma" literally means action and is a general feature of many Asian-based religions. For the Jains, karma is a material principle that drags down the soul. All our activities in the world drag down and limit a person's soul, leading one's soul to be reincarnated in the world. Hence, if one withdraws from the world, it is possible to receive the knowledge necessary to be freed from materiality.

Morality, along with quietism (and very strict asceticism), is the path to liberation from karma and rebirth. For the Jains, this kind of life is really only possible for monks and nuns. An essential aspect of Jain morality is to respect the life (soul) in all living things, from humans all the way to the insects and atom-sized souls. The Jain monk or nun is thus required to wear a mask to avoid accidentally swallowing an insect and required to sweep the ground as he or she walks so as not to walk on living things. Lay people cannot reach liberation, as they are too involved in the world and must await rebirth as a monk or nun to succeed. The moral rules thus are more relaxed for lay people, although they cannot be involved in the military or be butchers or take any job that involves killing living things. Many are thus involved in business and trade.

Our response to Jainism is as follows. We admire the commitment of Jains, especially the monks and nuns. The life they choose is arduous. We affirm, too, the pacifism that follows from the overall commitment to the affirmation of life of all sorts. We recognize that not all Christians are pacifists, but it turns out that we both are. Although we would reject the notion that the world is eternal and not created, we affirm that what is living seems to fall into a different sort of camp than do nonliving things. That's one of the mysteries of the world. What makes something alive as opposed to not alive? What is this "thing" called life? The Jains draw a very strict line between the living and the nonliving and draw that line by following a sort of dualism between the material and the spiritual. What makes something alive is its "soul" or "spiritual monad." We find this rather radical dualism, at least when drawn on those grounds, not to be complex enough to truly explain various levels of consciousness. Also, from a Christian point of view, we reject the extreme asceticism of Jainism. We believe that material things (including the nonliving) were made by a loving God who values all of creation. While some Christians (past and present) seek to free themselves of the material world (following, we believe, a too-strict platonic interpretation of Christianity), Christianity itself does not teach that the material world is bad but rather that it is good. When God created the world, as described in the first few chapters of Genesis, everything was pronounced good, not simply the living. But that raises the question, again: what are we humans? How is the human soul related to the material body? The religions historically rooted in Asian countries tend to downplay the material things of this world as being bad or less real than the spiritual.

BUDDHISM

We now come to Buddhism. The first and founding Buddha (there are others) was born and given the name Siddhartha Gautama. According to one story of his birth, he is said to have lived in one of the Buddhist heavens, and when it was time to be born, he came into human life through the womb of queen Maya. He was born to a rich and privileged family, but as he grew older and was exposed to the suffering of other people, he left the comforts of home to seek the truth about the world and life. He studied with a number of yogis and religious teachers, practicing severe asceticism, but did not find the truth he sought. Upon being severely tested by Mara (the Buddhist equivalent of the devil), Gautama put himself into a trance and went through a number of stages of meditation, the last of which provided Enlightenment, and Gautama became the Buddha, the "Enlightened One."

From this experience, he taught what have come to be known as the Four Noble Truths and the Noble Eight-fold Path. The Four Noble Truths are (1) the truth of suffering, (2) the source of suffering (which is desire), (3) the cessation of suffering (by the cessation of desire), and (4) the Noble Eight-fold Path as the means to the goal of the cessation of suffering. The Noble Eight-fold Path came to be known as the Middle Way, namely, the middle way between Jain extreme asceticism and worldliness. The path includes (1) right understanding, (2) right-mindedness, (3) right speech, (4) right action, (5) right livelihood, (6) right effort, (7) right meditation, and (8) right emancipation. The first two deal with the proper understanding of truth and the appropriate attitude, the next three make up the moral framework for Buddhism, and the final three steps provide for the mental disciplines that, based on the previous five, prepare and direct the person to achieve nirvana.

There are, of course, mountains of literature on these various aspects of the Buddha's teaching. We can only be brief. Right understanding includes seeing that suffering is everywhere; life is permeated with it. All suffering has its source in grasping or craving or burning thirst (desire is really too weak a term) after worldly things. For suffering to end, one must lose one's burning thirst for things of the world. The path from suffering is the Noble Eight-fold Path.

Suffering leads to rebirth. Buddhism extends the notion of karma from the materialist Jain notion to a much richer, psychological notion. How we act in this life shapes and influences how we are in the next life. But one must be careful here. It is easy to think of rebirth as reincarnation, as if there is a more-or-less eternal soul that continues from one life to another. For the Buddha, there really is no soul *per se*. Rather, a person is a collection of psychological states—perceptions, ideas, experiences, and so forth. (This might remind you of David Hume from chapter 2. There is plenty of fertile ground for comparison!) Strictly speaking, in Buddhism one has no soul, but one is made up of a collection of psychological states. One's present states cause one's future states. This is the Buddhist understanding of karma—actions carry influence from one life to another. So in Buddhism, karma leads to rebirth rather than reincarnation strictly speaking. This point is important because, in later Buddhism, a number of different interpretations of this doctrine tended to divide Buddhism into several schools. Unfortunately, we can't take the space here to discuss all the interesting ins and outs of those developments.

The Buddha's teaching about the nature of the self does lead to something we must discuss. *Nirvana* (which means "cooling off" or "going out" like a flame does) becomes problematic on the Buddha's teaching. Is the Buddha in nirvana or not? That is, what happens to the person when he or she reaches Enlightenment? Since there is no eternal self, what is the state of the Enlightened person? Buddhists usually reply as follows. There are two stages: nirvana with substrate (which is what happens to a person who has reached Enlightenment while still alive on earth—a state of peace and insight) and nirvana without substrate, which is what occurs upon an Enlightened one's physical death. An Enlightened one will not be reborn, so what happens to the person? The *arhat,* or Buddhist saint, it appears, cannot enjoy an individual nirvana. It is not like the Christian heaven, where individuals are in the presence of God. For the Buddhist in nirvana without substrate, there is no individual. So the question "is the Buddha in nirvana?" cannot be answered. In fact, the question cannot really be asked. It is like asking which direction a flame goes when it goes out—is it north, south, east or west? The question is, really, a sort of nonsense question.

The final aspect of Buddhism we want to note deals with the question of *bhakti*, which is, basically, religious devotion to a god (including obtaining favor toward nirvana). The Buddha was not considered a god. Buddhism is, like Jainism, fundamentally atheistic. The older, more traditional form of Buddhism, known as *Theravada* Buddhism, continues with this notion. However, Theravada Buddhism tends toward a sort of quietism, or withdrawal from worldly affairs, in how the Buddhist should live. Once someone has reached nirvana, what is the point of reaching out, living the life of compassion toward others? In response to this quietism, some developed the tradition of honoring the Buddha as if he were nearly a god, with statues of the Buddha, and eventually the development of the notion of a *bodhisattva*. A bodhisattva is a Buddha (or an "almost Buddha") in a sense extending beyond what Theravada Buddhism taught. In Theravada Buddhism, only the Buddha *before reaching Enlightenment* was a bodhisattva. In the later school, known as *Mahayana* (Greater Vehicle) Buddhism, the bodhisattva is any person who, when nearly reaching nirvana, allows him- or herself to be reborn. This generates a sort of merit, which can then be accessed by humans in the suffering world. Thus, in Mahayana Buddhism, there are a great number of bodhisattvas who are honored or worshiped nearly as if they are gods. In this way, the more ordinary Buddhist can gain grace in order to be closer to entering nirvana. This opens a path to the notion of honoring the bodhisattvas by acting compassionately toward other persons, thus leading away from a strict life of quietism.

Once again, there are a great many details and different schools (Chinese and Japanese versions of Buddhism, for example) we are passing over. But we must press on. What do we think of Buddhism? Again, we admire the emphasis on peaceable living and compassion. Many Buddhists are, in fact, very compassionate. We think the world can use more pacifists too. We admire the richness of the thought that Buddhism contributes to philosophical work, along with the meditational approaches, which overlap in many ways with Christian meditational practices. Finally, we admire the emphasis on what is called "mindfulness." We haven't discussed this notion, but it includes a way of accepting what comes one's way, of living in the moment, and being at peace with the world. We think it is significantly parallel to living in Christian joy and thus want to praise it. One of your authors occasionally thinks that if he weren't a Christian, he might be able to be a Buddhist. However, then he compares the Buddhist idea of self to the Christian idea of self and realizes he could not change his beliefs enough to make the shift.

We don't think the account of the Buddhist person is "thick" enough. We think there are good reasons to not separate the human body from the human spirit or mind. Not, of course, that we want to reduce the human spirit or mind to the body—we know that from chapter 3. We also affirm the mystery that is free will. But we also affirm, as Christians, the deeply biblically rooted notion of the human person as a psychophysical unity. When God created the first human, God scooped together dirt and then breathed the divine breath into the dirt and "it became a living soul." Buddhists would say they don't really separate the human spirit and the body. Indeed, they say, a person *consists in* the psychological and physical experiences of the human. We find the biggest challenge to Buddhism in its inability to explain what happens after the final, post-Enlightened death of a person. The Buddha says we can't really ask. If the Buddha were right about the true nature of the human person, perhaps he was right about not asking. But we find ourselves wanting a little more "post-mortem" life than Buddhism seems to allow. The individual self seems just to disappear in the Buddhist nirvana.

Of course, the Buddhist might just say our desire for a post-mortem individual existence is simply part of the overall desire that causes suffering in the first place. We, too, affirm that desire or attachment to the things of this world can lead to a great deal of suffering. However, we believe that Christianity has a clear enough emphasis on self-denial to handle that problem without requiring that the human individual simply disappear at some point. We don't, in fact, see why the cessation of desire is itself necessarily a good thing. Some desires, such as those for the good health of another person, are good desires. The desires to love and be loved can be good desires. Selfish desires are not, we think, good things. Yet it seems that to make sense of good desires one must also have a self that continues, and that self needs to be acknowledged as more than a bundle of psychological states.

HINDUISM

We turn next to Hinduism. Here we can again only briefly describe certain themes. The first is that in Hinduism there are two important streams, the yogic and the *bhakti*, that is, the contemplative and the worshipful. There are, as well, two streams of scriptures, the *Upanishads* and the epic poems, the most important aspect of which is the *Bhagavad-Gita*. These are complex scriptures containing many different and often paradoxical claims. The contemplative and the worshipful traditions emphasize different components of these scriptures. The older tradition is the yogic with its emphasis on contemplation. This stream focuses on the notion of Brahman or ultimate reality. Its roots are in the early sacrificial system of the Vedic religions. As the idea of the sacrifice developed, not only were the sacrifices and the priests (also referred to as Brahman or Brahmin) sacrificial but also eventually the whole of the cosmos was seen as sacrificial. In the *Upanishads*, the doctrine of rebirth is first announced along with the idea of using contemplative techniques to free oneself from the wheel of rebirth. This finally led to the notion of "That thou art" or the idea that the individual self and the ultimate reality of the universe share the same essence. "Atman (the human individual) is Brahman (the ultimate reality)." The realization of this truth was found via contemplation and yoga. In these versions of Hinduism we see the emergence of the idea that ultimate reality is above the gods, along with everything else.

Later, in the development of the *Gita* traditions (and in the *Upanishads*), the notion of worshipping one or another of the many gods comes to the fore. Thus in classical and later medieval Hindu traditions, various schools of thought arose. Before we consider those, however, let's note that in the *Gita*, there is a shift in the notion of karma. In Jainism, it is action itself that binds one to one's karma (leading to rebirth). But in the *Gita*, Krishna (who is an incarnation of the god Vishnu) teaches Arjuna (the main character in the *Gita*) that it is not action that binds one to karma but rather binding oneself to the result of the action. If one can learn to not be attached to the good (for oneself) that comes out of an action, one can be free from karma and hence free from rebirth. Everything should be done righteously but one should remain unattached to any good that results from living righteously. Hence there is a sort of good works (done to others), which are the result of faith. Salvation thus comes by faith.

The two main gods of Hinduism are Shiva and Vishnu. These gods are thought to be ways of expressing the ultimate truth about reality. It's not that there are two gods, exactly, but rather God may be worshiped either as Vishnu or Shiva. But Hinduism is also open to the existence of many gods. Hinduism, in a way, is the religion of thousands of gods. The *bhakti* traditions deal with the questions of how to worship the gods. We won't go into any further detail about Hindu worship except to note that much Hindu philosophy and theorizing deals with how the worship of gods and the notion of Brahman (ultimate reality) can be understood. We'll cover a few early interpretations and a few medieval interpretations.

Among the classical views are Samkhya, Mimamsa, and Vedanta. The first sees reality as the cosmos, which is a unitary being that evolves into the many forms we see around us, including innumerable eternal souls. The aim of the yogi, in this context, is to attempt a disentanglement of the souls in the cyclical rebirth (*moksha* or liberation). The soul can only be at peace when freed from the cosmos and all its suffering. Mimamsa is quite different in that it rejects the notion of *moksha* and emphasizes the notion of heaven where righteous souls go. If one does the appropriate sacrifices, one goes to heaven. However, Mimamsa is atheistic. Finally among the classical approaches is Vedanta. It emphasized belief in the single reality (Brahman).

There are many medieval systems of Hindu philosophy as well. Three of the main ones are versions of Vedanta. Their founders were Shankara, Ramanuja, and Madhva. The school following Shankara is called "advaita Vedanta." Shankara emphasized the relationship between humanity and Brahman as nondualistic, that is, he emphasized the claim that atman is identical to Brahman. It follows from this view that what we see around us is, in fact, illusory. There is, in fact, a single reality and what we see around us is imposed on that reality by us. So, strictly speaking, in *moksha* one does not become Brahman. One already is Brahman. There is no separate soul. Some of our readers may note some similarity here to the teachings of the Buddha. It is on precisely this point that other Hindu theorists reject advaita Vedanta. Ramanuja questioned whether it made sense to worship one of the gods, say Vishnu, while at the same time recognizing that one is identical to Brahman. Isn't that rather like worshiping one's own self? So according to Ramanuja, the relationship between God and the world is rather like the relationship of the soul to the body. His position came to be called "Qualified Non-Dualism." Reality is, as Shankara said, a unity or whole, but in contrast to Shankara's teaching, for Ramanuja, reality has qualifications or distinctions. The cosmos is not an illusion in Ramanuja's thought.

The last version of medieval Hinduism we'll discuss is that of Madhva or Dualism. He taught a clear distinction between God and the cosmos, including humans. He comes out very strongly on the side of worship (*bhakti*) and thus emphasized the individual soul and its distinction from God. Among Hindu interpretations, his view is the closest to theism. Madhva also taught that because there are individual souls, there are also different kinds of heavens and hells. In fact, he even taught a sort of predestination, according to which some souls inevitably go to heaven, and others to hell. In most Hindu teachings, hell is a temporary place where one might go to work off one's karma. In Madhva's teaching, hell can be a more permanent place.

It is important for us to emphasize that all these views are orthodox or true and acceptable Hindu teachings. Thus we can see how vast and broad Hindu teaching is. Accordingly, assessing Hinduism is very complex. We will keep our comments brief.

We affirm the deep sense of mystery in Hinduism and the struggles among Hindu thinkers trying to sort out the relationship between humans, the rest of the cosmos, and ultimate reality. Insofar as some branches of Hinduism are theistic, we affirm them—with a very important difference: we affirm the existence of only one God. In the end, we don't find palatable those streams of Hinduism in which the individual soul doesn't exist (as we noted in discussing Buddhism). For one thing, if there are no individual souls, what is the basis for morality? We do not find the atheistic versions of Hinduism to be the best way to think about the world and where it came from. We affirm the idea of the role of faith (as one finds in the *Gita*). However, we find the notion that one can, perhaps, bring oneself to salvation via one's own efforts uncomfortable. Neither one of us thinks it likely that we can work ourselves or discipline ourselves sufficiently to free ourselves from our sin. However, we do affirm the shift in the notion of karma from action alone to a desire to free oneself from praise for acting well. Finally, we find it hard to wrap our minds around the notion that everything except Brahman is illusory.[1]

CONFUCIANISM

Confucianism derives its English name from Confucius, which is a Latinized version of "K'ung-fu-tzu" which means "Master K'ung." K'ung was born in the Chinese province of Lu around 558 BCE and died around 479. He may have had aristocratic roots, although it seems that his immediate family was rather poor. He became a minor government official, however, and acquired considerable education. He became a teacher of *li* or ceremonial. Ceremonial had to do with etiquette and how a gentleman should act. Formerly the prerogative of the aristocracy, K'ung's teaching of *li* extended gentlemanliness to everyone. His influence in China is immeasurable, including the shaping of the social order and opening civil service exams to everyone.

There are five classic Confucian texts, *Ch'un Ch'iu* (Spring and Autumn Annals), *I Ching* (Book of Changes), *Shu Ching* (Book of History), *Shih Ching* (Book of Poetry), and *Li Chi* (Records of Ceremonial). Along with these are the four books, *Lun Yu* (The Analects), *Ta Hsueh* (Great

---

1. As a final note, we want to point to contemporary versions of Hinduism that are influenced by Christianity and the theism of the Middle East, especially the Hinduism of Ram Mohan Roy and Mahatma Ghandi. But we simply don't have time to discuss them here.

Learning), *Chung Yung* (Doctrine of the Mean), and *Meng Tzu Shu* (Book of Mencius). We will not go into details of these works except the Analects, which most easily represents the teaching of K'ung. Mencius is also an important teacher of Confucianism, but we simply can't cover everything.

K'ung was a genius at drawing out and extending the values of a tradition. There are a number of key concepts. We'll begin with *li*. The term means "ceremonial" but could be translated as propriety or reverence. The emphasis here is on how one should present oneself, how one should act around others. Reverential propriety meant much to K'ung, because he believed that the disordered and distressing situations of society are due not to the innate evil in the human person but rather to a lack of social cohesion. The term *li* originally dealt with the ceremonial of the religious life, but K'ung extended it to include all social interactions.

This brings us to the second important concept: the five relationships. These are father and son, elder brother and younger brother, husband and wife, elder and younger, and finally ruler and subject. The second of each of these pairs was thought to be inferior in status to the first of the pair. Thus, the son should show filial piety and the father kindness; the younger brother should show respect, the older brother nobility; the wife should show obedience, the husband care; the younger should show deference, the older humaneness; and finally, the subject should show loyalty and the ruler benevolence.

When these relationships are properly balanced, *jen* (the innate capacity for goodness and harmony in the individual—what we might think of as virtue) emerges. When proper reverence is shown, the ills of society, including the coarseness or meanness of the individual human, will be overcome by harmony and goodness. At the very heart of all this is *shu,* or reciprocity. This one word was thought to sum up all the rules of practice for one's life and was captured by K'ung in the saying, "What you do not want done to yourself, don't do to others."

The final concept we want to mention is *Tao,* or the Way. (Here we must caution the reader not to confuse this notion with the same term used by the Taoists, who understand something quite different by the term). K'ung sometimes used the term by saying "the Way of Heaven." K'ung's concept of heaven was no doubt shaped by the more traditional Chinese concept of heaven, which is bound up with the idea of a supreme providential being as well as the notion of good. K'ung espoused the notion that, rather than being determined by heaven, we should wait upon the decree of heaven. That is, heaven favors the good, but adversities occur in our lives.

One question often raised about Confucianism is "just how religious is it?" While it is possible to read Confucianism as not religious, the notion of heaven is clearly extra-natural and K'ung appeals to it, it seems, in straightforwardly religious ways. He taught not just ceremonial for the living but for one's ancestors as well. However, he did seem concerned that people might get overly entangled in religious matters and forget the importance of society. When asked how one should serve the spirits he once replied that we don't yet serve one another, so how can we serve the spirits?

Our response to Confucianism is brief. First, we very much admire the emphasis on good, reverential social interaction. We affirm, too, the notion of a supreme providential being and the notion of *jen*, which we take to be an account of virtue or flourishing. However, we are concerned with the apparently conservative social ordering of superior place to inferior place. Although Confucianism does emphasize what we might summarize as love from the supposed superior to the inferior, we wonder if that is enough. What hope does Confucianism offer to poor and uneducated persons? Further, we see very little explanation of the actual nature of the human person other than the claim that humans have innate goodness. (Other Confucians, such as Hsun Tzu, thought humans were essentially bad. Again, we don't have the space to deal with all the ins and outs of Confucian history.) But what of the body and the soul? Do we go to a place called heaven after we die? Is it possible for human beings to interact with God?

JUDAISM

We turn now to the theistic religions of the Middle East. Judaism's roots are as complex as any other religion. One thing that distinguishes Judaism from most other religions (except for Christianity, which grew out of Judaism) is its historical nature. What we mean is that in both Judaism and Christianity, God is understood primarily as the God who acts in history. Of course, history alone cannot show that a religion is true. The fact that Sarah and Abraham, for example, were historical persons and that they believed they held a covenant with God does not show, by itself, that God actually covenanted with them. But nonetheless, history is central to Judaism. Judaism points to the importance of a number of people in its history: Abraham and Sarah, Moses, Esther, Elijah, Isaiah, Jeremiah, and others. Judaism holds that God revealed the divine self to various people in history, first calling Abraham and Sarah out of Ur to the promised land, later leading their heirs to Egypt in a time of famine only to free them in the Exodus later through the guidance of Moses. Moses was the recipient of the law, and later there were important developments and interpretations of the law. Early on, God was understood as the one who covenanted with his *people* Israel. Later the themes shifted to a more personalized relationship between God and individual humans, as found in the teaching of some of the prophets. Throughout Israel's history, one important theme is the struggle of the Jews to shed themselves of polytheism and idolatry. The cultures surrounding Abraham and Sarah were polytheistic, the land of Canaan to which they were called was polytheistic, and later, after Moses and the return of the Israelites to Canaan, the Jews continued to struggle with keeping themselves purely monotheistic. It is not until after the exile (during which time, Jerusalem was conquered and many of the ancient Jews were forced to move to Babylon) that Jewish culture became clearly and totally monotheistic.

A number of other themes could be emphasized as well, but perhaps the most important are these. First, God is understood as a personal being who created the universe, including humans. While there are clear themes found in the early chapters of the book of Genesis that overlap with other ancient near Eastern cultures (such as a flood story and the loss of eternal life), one of the distinctives of Judaism is that humans did not have to earn eternal life with God but rather were created with it. Humanity fell from this relationship with God not because of ignorance or trickery but because of humanity's decision to disobey God. This aspect of the Jewish story emphasizes the importance of morality in human life. The second important theme is the centrality of the scriptures for Judaism. We won't go into details, but the Jewish canon (the books accepted as scriptural) was finalized by the end of the first century CE. The Hebrew Bible consists of the same books accepted later by the Christian church as Old Testament. But the Jewish tradition also includes a large set of documents called the Talmud. The Talmud is made up of various rabbinic (from the term for teacher, Rabbi) interpretations of the scriptures that have evolved over many years.

A third theme is the importance of the law for the Jewish faith. The law of God, given to Moses, provides the basic framework of life for more traditional or Orthodox Jews. (There are also Reformed Jews who, like some Christians, have been deeply influenced by the modernist challenges to the authority of the scriptures.) A Jew's life in relationship with God is one that (before the destruction of Jerusalem and the dispersion of the Jews throughout the Mediterranean and later Europe and the world) centered on the sacrificial system at the Temple. After the destruction of the Temple, Jewish life and worship centered on the Synagogue and the keeping of the law and various religious celebrations, including Passover, Yom Kippur, Purim and Hanukah. Various dietary laws and laws dealing with rest on the Sabbath are to be kept. For many Jews, the keeping of the law is the central religious duty. Keeping the law is the means via which one stands in good relationship with God. In early Judaism there is little talk of an afterlife, hence the focus of following the Law was not on a next-world salvation but rather the appropriate way to live one's life in the here and now. However, by the first century BCE, there is a good deal of talk of the afterlife, including an emphasis on the possibility of resurrection. During this same time period, certain biblical passages were interpreted as predicting the coming of the Messiah who was (and is) understood as a human who will act for God in restoring the Jewish people to peace and prosperity. In most Orthodox and Reformed Jewish celebrations of the Passover, the Messiah is remembered and looked for.

Another central event for the Jews, and one we must not forget, is the Holocaust, when approximately six million Jews were slaughtered under the Nazis in Europe. This led, in part, to the huge movement of Jews back to the land of Israel. For some Jews, it led them deeper into their faith. For others, it was the final straw in a long history of persecution and they left the faith.

Our response to Judaism is as follows. As Christians, we recognize the deep debt Christianity owes to Judaism. From Judaism we received the centrality of God in our religious beliefs. The Jews gave us the biblical concept of God—an everlasting, overwhelmingly powerful, wise, and morally perfect Creator of the universe. We also received, with substantial modification, our notion of the Messiah, the Christ, who came to save the world. The Jews, however, do not primarily think of the Messiah as a divine figure but rather as a human person endowed by God to bring an earthly redemption. Christians believe the Messiah has come in the person of Jesus who is both human and divine. We also received from at least one early branch of Judaism (the Pharisee sect) the doctrine of the resurrection of the body. While Orthodox Judaism by and large thinks of Christianity as a separate religion, Christians tend to think of Christianity as an extension or completion of God's ancient dealings with Israel. So your authors think quite highly of Judaism, although we think the Messiah has already come in the person of Jesus.

ISLAM

The last religion we will consider is Islam. Mohammed was born about 570 CE. Prior to Mohammed, Arab culture had largely been disrupted by war. Arab religion was polytheistic, although it did recognize a supreme God, Allah. Mohammed was influenced both by Judaism and Christianity. When he was 40 years of age, he began receiving visions and other experiences of the presence of God, which were recorded in the Qur'an. From the point of view of Islam, the Qur'an is the infallible word of God. Its poetry is quite beautiful and it deeply shaped the Arabic language. In addition to the Qur'an, there is the Hadith, a series of statements or communications about the life of Mohammed. It is divided into three "levels": sound, good, and weak, depending on the strength of the evidence for the authenticity of the statements (as decided by Islamic scholars during the generations shortly after Mohammed's death).

Mohammed conceived of God as a majestic unity. God is both righteous and merciful. It is blasphemous to offer worship to any being but Allah (God). In addition to this basic conception of God, Mohammed saw himself as the last in a line of prophets leading from the Hebrew prophets, through Jesus, to himself. Besides God, there are angels (created beings who carry out God's desires). One angel, Iblis, (the devil) and his agents obstruct the work of God, but only as Allah allows. Islam includes a doctrine of the afterlife in which some are sent to hell and eternal torture and others to heaven and eternal bliss. Only those living a righteous life go to heaven. Jesus is thought of as a prophet of Islam. The Qur'an denies that Jesus died on a cross (there was a substitute instead) but does claim that he was born of a virgin and that he will return again, although not as a judge. Only Allah can judge. Jesus is not the Son of God. Being a Son of God implied in Mohammed's context a physical cause for a son, so Islam rejects the Fatherhood of God.

There are five pillars of Islam. The first is the repetition of the brief creed: "There is no god but Allah, and Mohammed is his prophet." The second is prayer, which the faithful do five times a day facing Mecca. The third is almsgiving, the forth fasting (during the month of Ramadan), and the fifth the pilgrimage to Mecca (if a Muslim's circumstances permit). There are some strict ethical teachings as well, including having a right attitude (external action is not enough) and the prohibition of gambling, wine, and pork.

There is, again, much more to Islam and Judaism than we have mentioned here—a great deal of ethical teaching, for example. But we must close our discussion with a few notes on our response to Islam. Islam is theistic with a God who created the world, including humans. There is a clear emphasis on living an ethically good life, bringing into alignment how one acts externally with one's internal attitude. These we take to be good things. However, we do not accept the Islamic rejection of the Christian doctrine of the Trinity, which is implied in the rejection of Jesus as the Son of God. Although not totally absent from Islam (God is conceived of as merciful), we also look for a stronger notion of what Christians call "grace."

In the next chapter, we will describe some basic concepts in Christianity and explain why we think being a follower of Jesus is the best way to deal with the mysteries of the universe that the various religions try to explain.

6

Finding Our Place in Christ: Why We Are Christians

Synopsis: In this chapter we give a short summary of basic Christian beliefs; we think virtually all Christians will agree with them. The reasons for faith vary from person to person, so each of us explains separately why he is a Christian.

As we said in chapter 1, we do not accept the traditional philosophical ideal of the lone thinker. It's just a fact about human beings that we are social beings, and our sociality affects our thinking. In particular, we recognize that the prayers and encouragement of other people nurture our religious faith. But our social nature is not the whole story. Each person, though influenced by other people, still must take responsibility for his own beliefs.

Therefore we write this chapter in two parts. Our reasons for being Christians overlap, but each one of us, Mark and Phil, speaks for himself.

WHAT IS A CHRISTIAN?

In chapter 4, we said that a religion could be basically correct and yet wrong on some detail or another. So we tried to describe and respond to the basic ideas of the religions, not the many variations and details. We find things to admire in each religion—at the very least, the religions recognize that human existence is mysterious, and they try to help us respond to mystery appropriately.

We must now take a similar approach to Christianity. That is, we will talk in broad generalities about the basic framework of Christian belief and practice, not the details that separate the branches of Christianity from each other. If we are going to say why we are Christians, we must first say what a Christian is. It seems to us the following is a fair initial description.

A Christian is someone who believes in God, that God made the universe, that God made human beings to inhabit a portion of the universe, that God desires a loving relationship with human beings, that God acted to establish loving relationships with human beings by living among them as the human Jesus, that human beings rebelliously killed Jesus, that Jesus rose from the dead, that God offers a loving relationship to any person who believes in Jesus, that God (in the person of the Holy Spirit) is present "in" and "with" people who believe in Jesus, and that at the end of history all of Jesus' people will enjoy a loving relationship with God forever.

That may seem like a lot, but really it's an extremely simplified version of Christian beliefs. In no way do we intend that our statement be taken as a full presentation of Christian beliefs. Christians in every church will want to add to our description. But we think it clear that any person who believes the things we listed is a Christian of one sort or another. Many readers will recognize that the previous paragraph recapitulates most of the affirmations of the Apostles' Creed; we're not trying to be original.

As we explained in chapters 4 and 5, our interpretation of "being a Christian" is inclusivist. We think that God offers salvation to human beings on the basis of Jesus' death and resurrection. It is quite possible, we think, that some persons could devoutly believe in the doctrines of other religions and yet be saved because of the grace of God extended to us through Jesus.[1]

PHIL SMITH

I am not going to try to give every reason I have for faith, nor will I explain lots of arguments for the truth of Christian beliefs. I'm going to focus on just two main points, because they have been the most im-

---

1. Though we think inclusivism is a better way to think about the relationship between the religions than its rivals (exclusivism or pluralism), we are clearly *not* putting inclusivism in the list of basic Christian beliefs. Lots of Christians are exclusivists or pluralists. Please recall that in our discussion of inclusivism in chapter 4 we emphasized that only God may judge the eternal destiny of any person.

portant in my own spiritual pilgrimage. I imagine and hope that other people will appreciate the persuasiveness of these two reasons, but it's always possible that someone could read them and go away unimpressed. Please, dear reader, if you find my reasons of little weight, don't stop here. Read Mark's half of the chapter. Read other apologists. You should not conclude that there are no good reasons for faith until you have thoroughly canvassed the field.

Before I discuss the two primary reasons for my faith, I first need to say something about the difference between causes and reasons as applied to beliefs. Most of us are committed to the belief that if anything happens, there must be a reason for it.[2] But if we are more careful, we will notice that "reason" (as used in the previous sentence) has two meanings. Sometimes we mean "cause" and sometimes we mean "reason." For instance, if the "thing that happens" is a baseball flying over the right field fence, we might say the "reasons" for this occurrence include the batter's swing, the wind blowing out to right field, the poor location of the pitch, or the manager's foolish decision to use that pitcher. In this case, it would be clearer if we spoke of the "causes" of the home run rather than reasons. In general, when we analyze *events* in the world, we believe there are causes for those events. If something happens, we think it makes sense to ask what caused it to happen, and even in cases where we can't yet identify the cause, we think it is proper to look for it.

On other occasions, though, we really mean "reason" when we say "reason." For instance, when you perform an arithmetical calculation (246 x 71, let's say) each number you write down will be justified by a reason. (In the "ones" column, the answer will have a 6, and the reason is 6 x 1 = 6.) In general, when we analyze *truths*, we believe there are reasons for those truths.

Now, *beliefs* are a bit strange, because we can analyze them in terms of both causes and reasons. A belief is an event in the sense that some person somewhere affirms the belief. Therefore, we sometimes analyze the belief in terms of the causes that brought about that person's affirming the belief. For example, suppose you were captured by a criminal

---

2. Philosophers call this the "principle of sufficient reason" (PSR). It can be expressed more precisely in one of three ways. (1) For any event x, if x occurs, there is a sufficient cause for x. (2) For any entity y, if y is real, there is a sufficient reason for the existence of y. (3) For any proposition z, if z is true, there is a sufficient reason explaining why z must be true. Notice that these three expressions of PSR practically invite confusion between causes and reasons.

gang whose goal was to convince you that the governor is a tyrant and should be assassinated. While you are in their power, they force you to watch hundreds of hours of propaganda tapes that detail the alleged evils of the governor. If, after many months of this treatment, you were convinced that the governor deserves death, we would say the cause of your belief is the brainwashing you received from the gang.

Here is a less dramatic example. I believe that Barack Obama is President of the United States. I came to have this belief in the same way hundreds of millions of other people did: I watched his inauguration on television. Since beliefs are events in the world, beliefs have causes.

However, to believe something means that you think it's true. (No one would say, "I believe this, but it isn't true.") Therefore we often analyze beliefs in terms of truth. As I said a few paragraphs back, when we analyze truths, we speak in terms of reasons.

Here is the point of this discussion of causes and reasons. When we talk about beliefs, it is quite appropriate to analyze them in terms of both causes and reasons. However, it is very important not to confuse the two. A *cause* for a belief tells you how you came to hold that belief. It is historically oriented. But a *reason* for a belief tells you why you hold the belief now. It is oriented to the present and future.

I am going to explain two reasons why I am a Christian. In chapter 1, I told a little bit of my journey of faith, which explains to some degree how I came to have my beliefs. But for our purposes in this chapter, I need to present my current reasons (some of them) for my beliefs. *How I got here* is not the same thing as *why I am here*.

The first reason I am a Christian is this. I think Jesus rose from the dead. According to the New Testament, the resurrection of Jesus is the crucial, most important claim in Christian theology. The first century Christian apostle, Paul, wrote that if it were not true that Jesus rose from the dead, then Christian faith is worthless (1 Corinthians 15:14). The early Christian sermons in Acts make Jesus' resurrection central to the faith. (See Acts 2:31, 3:15, 10:40, 13:37.) Now, if Jesus rose from the dead, that does not prove that all Christian beliefs are true, but it does prove the most important Christian belief is true.

Okay: why do I think Jesus rose from the dead? There are two lines of reasoning that make me think this, one having to do with history and the other with my own experiences. I'll look at the historical evidence first.

The philosopher Gary Habermas[3] has explored the historical line of reasoning. Habermas points out that on some questions related to Christian origins, virtually all historical researchers agree. This surprises some people, because they assume that the origins of Christianity must be shrouded in uncertainty and debate. But in fact there is practical unanimity about several facts among historians who have studied Christian origins.

First, Jesus was a real man who was crucified under Roman rule in Palestine, sometime between 25 and 35 CE. Some skeptical scholars in the eighteenth and nineteenth centuries tried to question this fact, but no serious historians do so anymore. Jesus' death can be most likely put near the year 30 CE.

Second, Paul wrote 1 Corinthians, a letter to a group of Christian believers in the Greek city of Corinth, sometime around 55 CE. The authenticity of some of Paul's letters in the New Testament has been questioned, but no scholars today would deny that Paul wrote 1 Corinthians, and no one doubts that it dates from the mid-50s. As I noted above, in this letter Paul insists that Jesus rose from the dead; if he didn't, then Christian faith is worthless. This is not a new idea, Paul reminds the Corinthian Christians; he taught them the resurrection doctrine when he preached the news about Jesus to them a few years before.

Therefore—and Habermas points out that this is a third point on which historians agree—the message about the resurrection *predates 1 Corinthians* by some years, at the least. Paul says (1 Corinthians 15:1–5) that he received the message of Jesus' resurrection from other people, people who were actually present in Jerusalem when Jesus was killed.

The question springs up: when did the doctrine of Jesus' resurrection first arise? It was clearly some years before 55 CE, but when?

Here is a fourth point of agreement among historians. Before he became a Christian, Paul (going by his Hebrew name, Saul) was an enthusiastic member of the Pharisee branch of Judaism. In fact, he was a leading persecutor of the followers of Jesus. We learn this from the book of Acts as well as from Paul's own letters, including Galatians. (Like 1 Corinthians, no one disputes the authenticity of Galatians.)

So: before Paul wrote 1 Corinthians he traveled as a missionary to Corinth. Before he traveled to Corinth as a missionary, Paul traveled

3. See, Habermas, *The Resurrection of Jesus* and Habermas and Licona, *The Case for the Resurrection of Jesus.*

as a missionary to Galatia (in Asia Minor). Before that he had been a leader of the church in Antioch (for at least a year). Before that he had spent time (years?) in Tarsus (Acts 11:22–25). Before that, he spent three years in Damascus (Galatians 1:17). And before that he was converted to Christian faith.

Habermas points out that historians dispute none of this. Therefore—a fifth point of agreement among historians—Paul became a Christian well before the year 40 CE. In fact, the year 35 seems likely closer to the truth. Therefore we can say with very great confidence that Paul was converted from persecuting followers of Jesus into believing in Jesus only a few years after Jesus was killed.

Notice: if Paul (Saul) was persecuting Christians in the mid-30s, two facts must be true. First, there were followers of Jesus testifying that he rose from the dead only a few years after he was killed. The book of Acts and Paul's own testimony in 1 Corinthians say that many of Jesus' followers saw him alive, on several occasions and in diverse locations, after he rose from the dead. The belief in Jesus' resurrection is allegedly based on eyewitness testimony. In the mid-30s, when Paul (Saul) was persecuting the believers, most of those witnesses were still alive.

Second, the followers of Jesus who claimed that he rose from the dead—and this only a few years after his death—suffered for their testimony. They lost their property, they were put in prison, and some of them were executed. (Saul was a leader in the persecution of the followers of Jesus, but he was not the only persecutor.)

Remember, none of this is disputed. On purely historical grounds, it is virtually certain that followers of Jesus believed in his resurrection and publicly proclaimed this belief only a few years (or months) after his death, and they did this in spite of high cost to them personally. Very few people are willing to suffer for things they know aren't true. Obviously, the followers of Jesus in the mid-30s really thought he was alive. Many of them said they had seen him alive.

Now, why would people believe Jesus rose from the dead? Non-Christians who examine Christian origins owe themselves some explanation for the belief of the early Christians. Why were these people so sure Jesus was alive?

I am not arguing that the Christian belief must be true because the followers of Jesus were willing to suffer for their belief. History gives us examples of people who have willingly suffered for beliefs that turned out to be false. The early Christians' willingness to suffer for their beliefs only shows that those beliefs were sincerely held. No one disputes that the early Christians were sincere in their belief that Jesus was alive.

But *why* were the followers of Jesus so sure he was alive? It will not do to say a legend had grown up and people came to believe it was true. Most of us think many beliefs in many religions came about that way: an ancient story told for aesthetic or theological reasons is later mistaken for history. But the time frame in this case—at most a few years and maybe only months—precludes that scenario.

Some have suggested that Jesus' followers suffered from mass hallucinations, perhaps induced by wishful thinking. But the stories of Jesus' resurrection appearances put him with individuals, small groups, and large groups at different times and in different places. Hallucinations are usually experienced by individuals. A "mass hallucination" might be possible at one time and place. But it seems extremely unlikely that the variety of resurrection appearances can be adequately explained as hallucinations.

A few people have suggested that Jesus didn't really die. Instead, he faked his death somehow—with the help of his disciples or the Roman soldiers—and then claimed to have risen from the dead afterward. There is absolutely no evidence for this idea, and if it were true it would not explain why the inner circle of Jesus' followers believed that Jesus had risen from the dead, since they would be the ones who helped pull off the deception. The only good reason to pay attention to such a bizarre theory is that it shows how creative people can be in trying to invent an alternative explanation to the most obvious one.

The facts are that in the mid-30s Jesus' followers believed in his resurrection, and they were so sure of this that they were willing to suffer for it. The easiest and most obvious explanation for these facts is this: some of the followers of Jesus actually saw him alive after his death.

As I said, the historical line of reasoning is the first of two that supports my belief that Jesus rose from the dead. The second line of reasoning will seem very different, because it arises from my own experiences, and it is very short, consisting of one premise and a conclusion. Premise: though I have never seen Jesus (no visions like Christian mystic Julian of Norwich, no appearances like Paul's), it seems to me that I have had spiritual experiences caused by the living Jesus. Conclusion: therefore, my spiritual experiences are evidence that Jesus is alive. Corollary: if he is alive now, he must have risen from the dead, since no one disputes the fact that he was killed in the first century.

Clearly, I am not unusual in this respect. Hundreds of millions of people alive today would report similar experiences to mine; that is, they would say they have had experiences of the risen Jesus. I should be clear: I am not appealing to other Christians' spiritual experiences as evidence that Jesus is alive. I am merely admitting that my spiritual experiences are ordinary. In no way do I claim to have special access to religious truth.

Many people would object strenuously to this second line of reasoning. They would say that I ought to know that my so-called "spiritual experiences" are easily explained in terms of human psychology and/or social influences. They would not deny that I have had experiences of one sort or another and that I have learned from other superstitious people to call these experiences "spiritual," but they would completely reject the possibility that my experiences are any kind of evidence for the resurrection of Jesus.

These objections are all based in modern naturalism. I readily admit that if modern naturalism is true, then my "spiritual experiences" ought to be explained in some naturalistic way. If modern naturalism is true, then I ought to seek such an explanation in some psychological theory like Freud's. (Well, not like Freud's, since his speculations in *Totem and Taboo* have passed from favor, but like recent evolutionary psychology.)

But I don't think modern naturalism is true. As we explained in chapter 3, there are plenty of reasons to be suspicious of modern naturalism. The world is far more mysterious than a worldview based on nineteenth-century physics would permit. Though I am an enthusiastic supporter of scientific research, I do not believe that science can present answers to the most important questions.[4] The really important questions push me to recognize the deeply mysterious quality of human life, something that modern naturalism tries to avoid.

So I am not persuaded by the objections of the naturalist. I do not deny that psychology plays a role in spiritual experience, but I don't think psychological and/or sociological factors "explain away" my spiritual experiences.

---

4. Examples of truly important questions: Why is there something rather than nothing? Why is it that math, a human creation, describes the real world? What is the true nature of love and beauty? What is a human life for?

Here's an analogy. Suppose someone said my "learning experiences" in school could be explained by psychology and/or sociology. I should agree, to an extent. Obviously, psychological insight can be a great help to teachers. But suppose someone went further and suggested that psychological and/or sociological factors explained away my so-called "learnings." I would protest that I did in fact learn things in school, and the psychological/sociological story of how I learned those things is in that sense irrelevant.

Therefore, I am not persuaded by modern naturalism to ignore my spiritual experiences. It seems to me that in some of those experiences I have encountered the living Jesus. So I count my experiences as evidence that Jesus rose from the dead.

I said at the beginning that I would give two reasons why I am a Christian. The first was that I think Jesus rose from the dead. The second reason is this: The moral vision of Christianity enables human beings to flourish.[5]

What I mean by "the moral vision of Christianity" is complicated and big. As a philosopher, I will spend my entire career working mostly in ethical theory with the goal of exploring some parts of the moral vision of Christianity. Nevertheless, I can give a short exposition of the main ideas.

Christianity teaches that God is good and God created the universe to be good. God created human beings to be like God, and God actively intervened in human history through Jesus to help us become what we ought to be: like God. God continues to act, primarily by means of the Holy Spirit, to help us become what we ought to be.

That's it. Sounds simple, right? That's because I expressed everything in the most general terms. If you think about it a bit, some complications and questions turn up. So I'll add a few comments. First, notice that

---

5. Recall our discussion of flourishing in chapter 2. "Flourishing" is the word contemporary philosophers typically use to describe what ancient philosophers would have called "the good life." Aristotle called it "happiness" (*eudaimonia*). By using the term "flourishing," contemporary philosophers hope to leave behind the specific visions of the good life in history; they don't want their understanding of flourishing to be confused with Plato, Aristotle, or Aquinas's notions. At the same time, philosophers today don't agree in detail on what "flourishing" means in practice; the word serves as an underspecified ideal. Each writer is free to fill in the details as he or she thinks best; others may agree or not as they like. As a Christian, I am content to use the term and supply my own details. Readers can judge for themselves whether the kind of life I describe really is a flourishing life.

when Christianity says that God is good, it differs from some religions. Some religions, like ancient Manichaeism, have both good and bad gods, equal in importance. Other religions say that the Highest Being is beyond morality, so that moral terms do not apply. Christianity boldly claims that the ultimate reality, God, is morally good.[6]

Second, notice that God created people with a certain intention: that they be like God. Since God is good, this means that God intends that human beings be good. (I know that these sentences sound almost childish, like E.T. speaking to the little girl, "Be good." Bear with me.) According to Christianity, God has intentions for us; it matters to God what kind of life we live. Christianity boldly claims that the moral quality of human life matters.

Third, notice that though God created us to be good and wants us to be good, human lives often are not good. There is a religious doctrine, the doctrine of the fall into sin, which explains how this came to be. For the purposes of the moral vision of Christianity, it doesn't matter much how human beings became sinners. The point is that we are sinners— that is, our lives often display moral failure. Since we can observe human cruelty and selfishness readily, the fact of human sin is easy to admit. Christianity claims that human lives are moral messes. (I didn't say "boldly" because hardly anyone will disagree.)

Fourth, notice that God intervened in the human story by means of Jesus to help us become what we ought to be. This means several things. (1) Jesus models moral excellence for us. (2) Jesus allowed the human race to "act out" our rejection of God by crucifying him. (To the question, "Who killed Jesus?" the right answer is, "We all did.") But Jesus rose from the dead and offers forgiveness to us, in spite of the fact that we killed him. (3) Jesus continues to work, through the Holy Spirit, in human hearts. Christianity boldly claims that God has acted and is acting to help us become what we should be.

Fifth, notice that there is a goal to human moral life. God intends that our character become like Jesus' character. (This is one place where a philosopher interested in the virtues can spend his entire philosophical career. What are the virtues of Christ? How can we understand them?

---

6. I should probably add that God is also good in other ways. E.g. God is beautiful. But I emphasize God's moral nature because I'm writing about the moral vision of Christianity.

How can we gain them, at least a little? And so on.) Christianity boldly claims that the moral goal of human life is to become like Jesus.

Perhaps that is enough. The point, remember, is that I think this picture of the moral life helps human beings to flourish. According to the Christian moral vision, every human being lives a life that is important. According to this vision, God has a goal for each one of us, and the Holy Spirit works in us to help us toward that goal. Therefore, we have good reason to hope that we will get better. According to the Christian vision, the moral goal toward which we journey is expressed in Jesus. With Jesus' example before us, the virtues we pursue will include love, joy, peace, patience, kindness, gentleness, and self-control.

Obviously, what I have said here is just a beginning. But it is enough to justify my claim that the Christian moral vision helps human beings to flourish. Christian faith helps people—more specifically, it helps me— live a good life.

So: why am I a Christian? Because I think Jesus rose from the dead and because the Christian moral vision helps me live the kind of life I ought to live. There are lots of other reasons I might give, but these two head the list.

MARK MCLEOD-HARRISON

Sometimes students ask me why I believe what Jesus taught and I reply, only partly tongue in cheek, that I believe it because it's true. Student response is typically a sort of groan. They want something more than a report that I think Christianity is true. They already know that, they say.

The student disappointment goes something like this. What they were asking for is not why I believe but why I believe it is true. We all know that in most cases, believing something is true does not make it true. (I say in most cases because there are exceptions, as when my believing something makes it true that I believe it—but that is a philosopher's point, if there ever was one!) What makes a thing true is the way the universe is, not simply that one believes it is true. (More formally, what makes "p" true is simply that p is.) Truth, we might say, is ontological rather than epistemological. In other words, truth has to do with the way things are rather than the way humans think or reason about the ways things are. So truth and rationality are not the same thing. Yet we strive, as much as we can, to have only true beliefs. Or at least we should strive only to have true beliefs. Why? Because we think truth is a valuable thing.

I want to make two points. The first is that when we think about the relationship of truth and belief, we typically think that for us to line up our beliefs with truth is to think rationally. We have a deep sort of human conviction that rationality will lead us to truth. Typically, for our beliefs to be rational there must be some sort of reason or evidence or ground for the truth of the belief. I, too, think this is roughly right. However, I think we must be careful about how we think about reasons, evidence and grounds. If we lean too heavily on the modernist position that Phil and I reject—the notion of the human as a pure, thinking thing—reasons, evidence and grounds will be understood improperly. Reasons, evidence and grounds are, I think, perspectival. That is, they depend upon the framework or perspective in which they are rooted. For me, on the really big, mysterious questions, the perspective is one of hope. I'll return to this shortly.

The second point is this. I've already said that truth is a valuable thing. But is it valuable just because it is truth or for some other reason? It seems that truth is worth having just because it is truth. But I think that the value of truth, at least on the big, mysterious questions, actually depends on some other assumptions we often make. I sometimes ask a student to imagine her- or himself deeply in love with another person. I ask the student to imagine the relationship with this significant other to be what brings the student great, nearly total happiness. I then tell the student to imagine that some friend knows that the significant other is cheating on the student. I then ask whether the student would rather not be told about the cheating so she or he can go merrily along the happy trail or be told the truth and lose the happiness. Nearly everyone says she or he would rather know the truth. While there are occasional exceptions to this result, they are rare. I think the reason for this general result is that most of us think, at some deep level, that truth and happiness are linked, but they are linked in such a way that "happiness" without truth wouldn't be real happiness. Most of us would rather not be duped even if the dupery leads to great happiness. Consider a different scenario. Suppose we knew *with certainty* that the reality of the universe were that we are actually on the rack and being tortured day and night forever, but we also knew that by flipping a switch we would become duped into believing we were having a very pleasant day at the beach. In this case, most of us would take dupery and happiness over the truth with unhappiness. This scenario suggests that happiness is a more fundamental value than truth. How should we reconcile these seemingly contradictory intuitions? In the first case we'd rather know the truth, even if it ruins happiness, but in the second we'd rather be duped. I think the answer is this. We value truth (at least about the big, mysterious things) because we think it will make us happy *in the long run*. The reason we believe that, it seems to me, is because one of the fundamental and structural features of being human is our belief, as Gabriel Marcel puts it, that the universe is in connivance with us. (Remember, in the second scenario, we know *with certainty* that we are being tortured forever; hope is ruled out.) We do not know the future, and since the future may be wonderful, the mysteries of the universe call humans into hope. Most of us persist in the belief that truth will lead to happiness. Or at least that's what we want. The hope that getting the truth will lead to happiness is a fundamental framework or perspective from which we work and, I believe, from which we should work. There is nothing embarrassing or weird or wrong about taking a hopeful look at the universe, *especially when it is so full of mystery.*

I noted in chapter 1 that much of my early experience of Christian faith and life in general was filtered through doubt. We talked earlier about different kinds of doubt. Doubt for me was plainly the suspicion—the fear, even—that Christianity simply wasn't true. I didn't thereby think I could become a Buddhist or Hindu or any other sort of religious person. We've already talked about some of the reasons why we don't hold the various religious views that compete with Christianity in the quest for truth. But in the end, for me I simply could never see that I could take the option of living into another religion. The reasons why Christianity might not be true so overlapped with the reasons why any religion might not be true that I simply didn't (and still don't) see any good religious alternative to Christianity. For me, the only other option—the only viable option—was a pure secularism. But the secular option seemed then, as it does even more now, totally bereft of meaning and meaningfulness. It became more and more clear, especially as I grew older, that meaningfulness and hope were linked. If secularism were the ultimate truth, I could certainly not see the point of hope, and therefore I could not see what the point of living was. Since I hoped, I thought

Christianity a very good option. And I did (and do) hope! I couldn't (and can't) help myself.

So because I hoped Christianity was true, I pursued the possibility of its truth with quite a lot of passion. My doubting became, in a way, the grounds for my search. I looked at the various arguments for belief in God but found myself never much impressed with the traditional arguments for God's existence. That is not to say that I think none of them work. I'm not a Hume or a Kant in that regard. I simply found (and continued to find) that most of them seem to derive what rational force they have from my life's context. I don't see them as providing some sort of abstract reasons that a person could see from the vantage point of some sort of intellectual neutrality. So my thinking moved toward explaining the human experience of the divine as a ground for rationality. That was the subject of my first book. There I argued, following Alvin Plantinga and William Alston, that religious experience grounds (rather than provides reasons for) theistic belief. I still think that is true. I'm much more impressed by my *sense* that God created the beautiful flowers than I am by an *argument* from the beauty of flowers to the existence of God, although such an argument has its charm. I found that the arguments for God's existence made the most sense in the context of my already formed belief rooted in the experience of God rather than providing reasons in their own right for belief in God. I take most of the theistic arguments as good explanatory tools given theism rather than as reasons *in the abstract* for theism.

There are also some decent arguments for the historicity of the resurrection of Jesus from the dead. I'm not convinced, however, that we can draw strictly theological or religious conclusions from those historical arguments alone. However, I think that the historical arguments for the historicity of the resurrection point out a really, truly weird fact. This guy, Jesus, appears to have come back from the dead! That's not some parlor trick, like we do now when someone dies on the operating table and the good docs bring the person back to life. Jesus was rotting already and came back unaided by any natural medical means. Still, although very impressive, I don't see that that proves that Jesus was or is God. (See, I told you I was a doubtful skeptic!) And yet there is something so rich and so powerfully mysterious in the resurrection that I think and I hope that Jesus really was and is God.

Instead of arguments of the detached, rationalist type as evidence for Jesus' teachings, I'm inclined to believe in Jesus (and specifically, that Jesus was and is God) because of my own experience. So here I want to share from my heart some of my experience. First, I have experienced grace. What I mean here is, in one sense, difficult to describe. Yet in another sense, it is not difficult at all. When I have failed to be truly human, God has loved me anyway. Some years ago, I watched a film about Mother Teresa with my students. When she was asked to sum up the Christian gospel, she said that the gospel is love. I asked my mostly Christian students if she was right. Most of them said yes, she was. But then they started to wonder. Doesn't the gospel have to say something about Jesus? Doesn't it have to say something about believing? Doesn't it have to say something about Jesus dying on the cross? Doesn't it have to do with Jesus' resurrection? What is the essence of the Christian gospel?

Well, I believe it is love. God loves me. God loves you. It's simple. Yet how God loves us makes up the truth of the Christian faith. God loves us through Jesus. God loves us by inviting us to the journey of belief. God loves us through the death and resurrection of Jesus. Grace is just another word for love. I believe, more than I believe anything else, that God loves me no matter what I've done, no matter how weak or stupid or mean I am. God loves me just as I am.

This grand love is fundamental and at the center of Christian teaching. The doctrine is in some ways a complex one but in other ways, it's not. It's the doctrine of the Trinity. Utterly unique to Christianity (although there are plenty of other "threes" in the various religions), the doctrine of God being at once a complete unity and yet also three co-equal divine persons is a doctrine whose central teaching is about love. The three divine persons of the Trinity simply love one another. Their life together as one united being and yet three persons is sometimes described by the term "perichoresis." I think of perichoresis as the divine dance of love, each member of the Trinity submitting to the others, trying to "out do" the others in love. This is a powerful image. God is (at the very core of the divine self) social. God could not be if God were not a socially united reality. Such unity is the basis for all human sociality and for all human love. This love is far greater and richer than we can completely experience. God is indeed mysterious! But the amazing, overwhelming, and glorious thing about God is that the very maker and creator of all that is, the God to whom I (and all of us) owe my very life, God, through Jesus by the power of the Holy Spirit, holds out the divine hand and invites us into the dance that is God's love. In this dance, we are known, completely and utterly and purely. This is what we are meant for, and it is this for which I hope.

I have experienced this love—this grace—numerous times. I experienced it in my initial experience of conversion. I experienced it in my family growing up. I experienced it when I fell in love, more than once. I experienced it with my late wife and her illness. I experience in it the healing power of my wife, Susan, now. I experienced it when I fell in love with my two children. I even experienced it in suffering.

Here it seems important to say something about suffering or the so-called problem of evil. It is true that theists of all sorts face the problem of evil. How could a truly loving and all-knowing and all-powerful God allow such evils to exist? Little children dying of painful diseases. Random tortures and deaths of all sorts. The problem of evil, however, is really a variety of problems, and there are a variety of solutions. There is something called the logical problem of evil, which most philosophers believe is solved by the free-will defense developed most recently by Alvin Plantinga.[7] I agree. The logical problem is solved. There is something called the evidential problem of evil that suggests that while evil is not logically incompatible with God's existence, the amount of evil seems to count as evidence against God's existence. As a philosopher, I think there are solutions here too, having to do partly with free will and also with our not knowing how to weigh out the "value" of evil over the "value" of belief in God. But for me, the real kicker of a problem is what is sometimes called the existential or pastoral problem of evil.

When I was a teenager, one of my best friends was Randy. He was born with muscular dystrophy, a terribly debilitating disease where one's muscles basically atrophy, becoming weaker and weaker until you die. Randy suffered with this disease until just recently when he passed away.

---

7. The logical problem of evil claims that it is impossible to combine three propositions: (1) God is morally perfect, (2) God created the world, and (3) Evil exists in the world. The free-will defense replies that it is possible for all three propositions to be true at the same time, if a fourth proposition is also true: (4) God created free creatures in order to obtain some great good in the world that could not be obtained without the existence of free creatures. The point of the fourth proposition is that if God created truly free creatures, God could not prevent them from doing evil (or else they would not be free).

He lived a very long time for someone with the disease. That's not necessarily a good thing. A long life when you feel tortured every day isn't obviously a good thing. Randy's brother had polio as a child, a disease that killed many children in the 1950s. His sister was born with some congenital back defects and had to undergo numerous painful surgeries. Randy's mother and father lived with all of this pain and suffering. Randy's dad, I think, had a hard time accepting all of this. I can't comment further about Randy's dad except to say that he was a funny, if somewhat irreverent, person whom I liked very much. But it was Randy's mother, however, from whom I learned much. Elfrieda was a faithful Christian until she died. I called her "mom" (as Randy called my mother). When I went away to college, Elfrieda was diagnosed with multiple sclerosis, a painful, debilitating disease that eventually led to her early death.

When I came home from college that first Christmas, I went to visit my "mom" in the hospital. I went to her room, looked around, and saw no one I recognized. I left the room to check the name at the door. Sure enough, I had the right room. I went back in and looked again at the terribly swollen person in the bed. Elfrieda looked twice her normal size. She was so swollen up that I hadn't recognized her. So I went in and we talked. I read her some Psalms, her favorites. I held her hand and prayed with her. When we were finished praying, she looked at me and asked, "Mark, why is God doing this to me?" I was eighteen years old, and in that question I was introduced to the existential problem of evil.

Why was God, in fact, doing this to Elfrieda? I do not know. The answer is one of the greatest of all mysteries. I know, however, that suffering is no better explained from a secular point of view. In fact, the notion of suffering itself makes little cognitive sense from a secular or naturalist point of view. Why say anything is evil at all, if all that exists are atoms falling through space? If we want meaningfulness, we have to accept the reality of suffering along with the other extra-natural mysteries.

That brings me to the story of my late wife. I can't go into great details here. Let's just say that her life ended in misery. She was diagnosed with lupus, another debilitating disease where the body basically attacks itself. Typically it is the kidneys but the attack can occur against the skin, the heart, the eyes and even the brain. It was affecting Becca's nervous system and her sense of balance. And she was depressed a good deal of the time. Her hopes of finishing her PhD in history were dashed. She taught part time the last two years of her life, but it took every ounce of strength for her to do that. Most people have no idea how difficult her life was. She died in June of 2001. She was 43.

But here is the strange and weird and mysterious thing. She became a more and more grateful person the more and more she suffered. And she loved Jesus more and more deeply. Her life of prayer became astonishingly rich. Yet in the end, she lost her hope. Not her love but her hope of ever becoming healthy again. She took her own life out of the despair that is the opposite of hope. Yet she did not lose her hope in God. In fact, I'm sure she saw herself as going straight into the arms of Jesus and the divine dance where she could dance without falling down. Grace reached out to her, I believe, even in her despair. Where is the answer to the existential problem of suffering? Elfrieda didn't know. Becca didn't know. But I believe they do now. And I have some ideas.

I believe that the Holy Trinity takes up evil and suffering and transforms it somehow into true and genuine goodness for those martyrs who suffer the evils of this life. The reason I think there is an answer to the problem of evil is that I believe Jesus himself experienced the evil we humans could dish out. He experienced it and, being not merely human but divine as well, he was able to engulf the evil—all the evil—of the world. I believe, in other words, that the universe is in connivance with us to bring about the good. In short, I believe in hope. But I want to be clear here. I believe not just in the hope that gets us mundanely through each day, although that too is a good thing. Rather, I believe in the great hope that is the Good News of Jesus Christ. I believe in the great hope that God so loved each and every one of us that Jesus came and died for us. I believe in the great hope that Jesus, as human, understands me, but that as divine, he provides the very means for my flourishing as a human person. In short, I believe that hope opens the door for true and genuine belief. And hope opens the door for love.

Just after Becca passed away, my son, who was then just 11 years old, asked me why God had taken his mom and why he should believe in a God who would do such a thing. At first, I told Ian I didn't know, but he persisted. But then came the answer: I did know that whether there was a God or not, his mom was still dead. Yet the difference between a world with evil and God and a world with evil and no God is that the world without God would be a lot lonelier. I like company and that is why I am a follower of Jesus' way. I don't know where this answer came from; it wasn't one I'd ever thought of before, but it still sounds right.

But not all of life is suffering and loss. There is wonder and amazement and love and learning and a million other things redolent with fun and mystery. There is the mystery of consciousness. There is the mystery of language learning, of which, as I watch my younger son grow, I am daily reminded. There is the mystery of the sacrament of marriage, in which I've had the privilege of participating twice. Susan, my wife since 2003, has loved me in new and wonderful ways. She has brought me healing in many ways, including healing from the grief of the loss of Ian's mom. She has been Jesus for me in helping me see not only the healing I need but the possibilities of being a more loving person, and the possibilities of living the Christian life more consistently in terms of peace and justice toward others. We laugh together too, and that is a means of grace. I see Jesus in her love for Micah, and Ian, and me. These are mysteries beyond reductionistic explanations: life outside the merely natural.

So I really and truly believe the way of Jesus is true. And I hope it is as well. I don't think that on the big, mysterious issues of life belief and hope are incompatible attitudes. Without hope, I simply would have no belief and, I think, no good reasons to believe. Without that hope, much of my experience in life makes no sense and life seems meaningless. I think the teachings of the Christian faith make a lot of sense of a lot of weird and strange things. I think the reality of God explains beauty because God is Beauty. I think the reality of God explains goodness, because God is Good. I think the reality of God explains truth because God is Truth. And I think it is all wrapped up in a wonderful, if sometimes hardly believable, story of a God who was so full of love that it spilled over into the creation of the world and finally the creation of each and every human person. Each of us was made in God's image, and we are meant to flourish in the light of God's love. We have each of us screwed up our lives. Moral wrongs are wrongs. Our failures as humans in regard to living morally upright lives are legion. There are personal failures and weaknesses, and here I have in mind not moral weaknesses but just plain old finitude. Yet God loves us. Without a personal God in whom to ontologically root goodness, I don't see much sense in the human drive toward understanding mystery, the core of which is a longing for meaningfulness.

I know something of my own fallenness. I know how black I am capable of being. I know how weak I am, not just morally but in terms of knowledge and understanding. I believe these weaknesses too are part of my fallen condition. How am I to live a meaningful life, then, a life of wholeness and flourishing? The answer, in short, is best told in a story.

As we'll discuss in the next chapter, stories are vital to human meaningfulness. I leave the theory until then. But I want to share one of my favorite stories. Many of you will know it. It is the story of the Velveteen rabbit. A little boy is given a toy rabbit, but at first the boy largely ignores it as it sits alone in the playroom. But the boy eventually remembers the gift of the rabbit and begins to play with it day after day. Eventually, he begins to sleep with the rabbit at night. One day the rabbit is left outside where some real rabbits see it and they act in a quite condescending manner toward the Velveteen rabbit, since it isn't real. The rabbit is taken back to the house where it asks the older and much wiser toys how it can become a real rabbit. The old skin horse tells the Velveteen rabbit that it will become real when it is loved enough. The boy becomes very ill and nearly dies. But he is brought great comfort by the presence of the Velveteen rabbit, who snuggles up next to the sick boy. The boy recovers but all of the sheets and bedclothes and the Velveteen rabbit have to be burned because of the germs left on them from the boy's illness. When they are taken out to be burned in the fire, all at once (through the magic of a fairy), the Velveteen rabbit becomes a real rabbit. Off it goes to live, forever, among the real rabbits. The Velveteen rabbit becomes real because it is loved enough.[8]

This story briefly gives us a way to understand how Christianity brings us healing and the possibility of flourishing. We become real, in the end, because we are loved enough. But no human can love us enough. Only God can do that. And that is why I believe that Jesus' path is the true one. And it is a grand story. It is the one to which we invite you as well. There is plenty of room for more real rabbits. In fact, there is room enough, in the divine playroom, for all of us to dance. Won't you take our hands and join the best dance you've ever been to?

8. See Williams, *The Velveteen Rabbit.*

7

How to Flourish: Vocation and an Integrated Life

Synopsis: In this chapter we explain how the Christian story allows people to live integrated lives, lives of vocation. We invite the reader to take up a Christian self-understanding.

SOCRATES CLAIMED THAT NO one ever intentionally does evil. We always act to achieve something we think is good; evil results because people mistakenly pursue the wrong things. They think those things are good when they really aren't.

Whether or not Socrates was right (we're not convinced), we think it's true that almost everybody *wants* a good life. They want things to go well for themselves and (usually) for other people. In a very general sense, achieving a good life is what philosophers call "flourishing." A crucial feature of a flourishing life is that it is integrated.

But disintegrating pressures abound in our culture, and many people do not know how to resist them. Overwhelmed by disintegrating pressure, some people live lives of quiet despair; others create disaster zones of violence, substance abuse, and/or exploitation of other people. In this chapter we suggest that vocation is key to integrated living, and we urge readers to see their own lives as under a divine call.

An "integrated" life is one that makes sense, primarily to the person who lives it, but also to other people who know her. An integrated person feels some degree of satisfaction when she contemplates the various parts of her life because they fit together. We can make the concept of integration clearer by giving examples of lives that lack integration.

Consider:

1. A married woman who has made conscious commitments to care for the interests of her husband and children—yet she engages in a series of extramarital affairs.

2. A certified public accountant whose profession prizes honesty, attention to detail, and fiduciary duty—yet he piles up huge gambling debts and embezzles from clients to pay them.

3. A talented young violinist who has won a significant scholarship to a prestigious music conservatory—yet she hates practicing and wishes she could stay home and clerk in a grocery store so she could be near her boyfriend.

4. A college professor who has satisfactory teaching evaluations and an impressive list of publications in his field—yet the only thing he really enjoys is fly-fishing on weekends.

5. A college student whose addiction to computer games prevents her from keeping up with her classwork.

We could invent more examples, but perhaps these few point to the problem. Lives like this are "out of joint"; the parts don't fit together. Sometimes "dis-integrated" lives are marked by sheer hypocrisy, as in the case of a preacher who publicly condemns certain sins while secretly engaging in those very things. In other cases, though, the lack of integration is subtler, as in the case of a young adult who drifts through a dozen jobs in as many years, not for lack of talent but because she can't generate any desire to do anything; neither work nor leisure matters to her. And sometimes people just "box off" different parts of their lives, as in the case of a Muslim who always attends Friday prayers at the mosque but works for a meat-packing company that specializes in pork; he would never buy or eat his company's products, but every day he helps to sell them. His "personal life" and his "business life" are totally distinct.

STRUGGLES TO ACHIEVE INTEGRATION

We believe people naturally desire to live integrated lives. They would like to see their lives as wholes, where the parts all cohere and where the totality has a purpose or meaning. Historically, many philosophers and religious leaders have tried to advise people as to how to find or build integration in their lives. For example, the ancient stoic philosophers taught that the whole universe is ruled by reason (*logos* in Greek); the universe is a cosmos, not chaos. Everything that happens has a cause and a purpose. Therefore, the stoics advised, human beings ought to adapt themselves to the underlying rationality of things. We bring ourselves grief when we try to override the *logos* of the world. According to stoicism, the wise person finds contentment in playing a modest and proper role in the world.

Now, stoicism may or may not sound attractive to you, but over the centuries some people found in it resources to integrate their lives. The stoic philosophers certainly offered their doctrines as a way for persons to find purpose and peace of mind. Stoicism saw the human need for integration and taught people how to find it.

Stoicism is just one example. Many philosophical movements (Platonism, Epicureanism, Hegelianism, etc.) have had this feature: they give the individual a way to see her life as having coherence and meaning. Obviously, the great religions do the same thing. In each case, the philosophy or religion helps people achieve integration by telling them how they fit into the overall scheme of the universe.

Modern naturalist philosophers inherited this project of offering integration to people, and many of them tried to do it. Karl Marx can be taken as an example. Marx was quite explicit about his commitment to modern naturalism. An atheist, he taught that all human history could be understood in terms of dialectical materialism. The irresistible forces of economic history, he claimed, would destroy industrial capitalism, leading inevitably to a socialist political economy. Such doctrines might sound pretty bleak for the individual, and in the twentieth century many critics attacked communism for exactly that; they said Marx's ideas led to a totalitarian state that ran roughshod over individual rights. But we should remember that, for millions of people, Marxist ideas provided a sense of dignity and purpose. Marxism encouraged this thought: "Even though I was born a peasant farmer or an unskilled laborer, my life has meaning because I am a living embodiment of the needs and desires of the proletariat. I am not just a meaningless lump; I am part of the coming revolution."

Unfortunately for modern naturalists like Marx, they were swimming upstream against a powerful current. At its core, modern naturalism teaches that the human species as a whole—and necessarily each individual member of the species—is in reality a cosmic accident. We simply are whatever the mindless process of natural selection has produced. And the same thing can be said of every other living organism.

David Hume deduced the implication of modern naturalism back in the eighteenth century. From the point of view of the universe, he said, the life of a human has no more significance than that of an oyster.

If it is really true that we have passed from the modern era to post-modernism, then the last gasp of modernism was mid-twentieth century atheistic existentialism. Jean-Paul Sartre and other existentialists told a generation of young intellectuals that they could *choose* or *create* meaning for their own lives. It would be "bad faith," they warned, if a person believed that her chosen path in life somehow reflected some ultimate truth; she ought to recognize that the only thing that conferred value on her choice was that she chose it. It would not matter whether she chose to be a bourgeoisie banker or a communist revolutionary. In either case, by making her choice she created a world of values, bourgeois values on one hand or socialist values on the other.

Our comments here apply only to atheistic existentialism. The nineteenth century father of existentialism, Søren Kierkegaard, was a Christian, and many later existentialists were Jewish or Christian believers. Theistic existentialists often emphasize and explore the difficulty—even anxiety, or dread—of committing oneself to the mystery of God without any knockdown argument that God is real or that God is good. But the theistic existentialists do not imagine that a believer's commitment to God *creates* God or goodness. In contrast, atheistic existentialism says that human freedom is truly radical; an authentic choice to be a banker makes capitalism good for the chooser, while an authentic choice to be a revolutionary makes capitalism evil in the chooser's world.

Existentialism, then, offered people a last, desperate route to an integrated life. A person's life could make sense just insofar as he willed it to make sense. But existentialism was both inconsistent and despairing. Inconsistent: if it is really true that I create values by my choices, why must I choose authentically? What if I prefer to live aimlessly, making no commitments to anything, like the characters in the postmodern comedy *Seinfeld*? Despairing: if the authentic life is one in which I live up to the values I create by my choices, what is the value of my life if I fail? Suppose I commit myself to the revolution, intending thereby to benefit the workers of the world; do I rob my life of value if I turn aside from revolutionary ardor to care for a spouse or children?[1]

---

1. One might say, from a Christian standpoint, that existentialism lacks a doctrine of grace. "Salvation" comes entirely by means of one's choice and action.

Wildly popular among college students of the 1960s and 1970s, existentialism has lost its cachet. So where do postmodern students turn for integration?

In many cases, we think, the answer is "nowhere." We know, of course, that some students do pursue integrated lives, organizing their lives by reference to traditional schools of philosophy or (more frequently) traditional religions. But many students, including some who loudly claim religious faith, seem to live disintegrated lives, lives bereft even of the desire for wholeness.

Philosophy bears only a portion of the blame. After all, most students don't study philosophy before they reach college. Instead, they pick up postmodern attitudes from the culture around them. We see students who are the prey of a consumerist culture; from their earliest years, they are the targets of *advertising* and *entertainment* influences that pressure them to fragment their lives into multiple roles.

Many people have observed that advertising functions to make us desire products and services. Once desire is awakened, advertising urges us to act on it. In the aggregate, it doesn't matter which product or service is desired; the intended effect of advertising is to get the consumer to consume. It should not surprise us that after eighteen years of training as consumers, many twenty-year-old students identify themselves with their desires. *Volo, ergo sum*: I want, therefore I am. Since desires change from day to day, so does personal identity.

In the last decade, the internet has multiplied entertainment options far beyond the possibilities of even the 1980s. (Weird Al Yankovic ridiculed television entertainment with his song, Cable TV, in that sedate decade. "Eighty-eight channels of ecstasy; I've got cable TV," he sang. How quickly reality has overwhelmed parody!) With the internet, all the old forms of entertainment combined—theatre, concerts, movies, books, radio, recordings, sporting events, television, etc.—become a small portion of the possible options for the twenty-first century consumer.

The sheer number of entertainment options begets bewilderment: so much to see, so much to do! Web surfers inhabit a world of infinite possibilities, all of which are superficially the same. Information, opinion, analysis, sports, humor, pornography, campaigns for politicians or social causes, and hucksterism—whatever their content, all internet sites compete for the surfer's attention. In every case the surfer plays the role of consumer, sovereignly choosing whether to visit or stay on any site.

We should not be surprised if some surfers judge them all primarily as entertainment.

Perhaps the ultimate (so far) version of internet entertainment is virtual reality and role-playing games. Here, surfers assume alternative identities, as many as they like. They move from role to role. And then, when they leave the computer monitor, they take up yet another role; their real life. But many game players frankly admit they prefer their online roles to the limitations of "reality." As we said in chapters 1 and 2, we seem to see more and more young people for whom life consists of multiple disconnected roles.

Don't misunderstand us. We have no particular brief against the internet, virtual reality, or role-playing games. As we emphasize below, we think creativity and play are wonderful human characteristics. But we think that in our current culture, technology has magnified the influence of advertising and entertainment, and we think these forces put disintegrating pressure on people.

In this section we have frequently mentioned "students," because your authors are professors and we observe students often. Obviously, though, advertising and entertainment influence people of every age in this culture. In a postmodern world, many people, not just students, struggle to find wholeness.

THE STRUCTURE OF AN INTEGRATED LIFE: NARRATIVE

In his influential book, *After Virtue*, the philosopher Alasdair MacIntyre[2] says that human beings make sense of their lives by telling stories. In particular, they tell stories about themselves to themselves. The structure of an integrated life will therefore be a narrative structure.

MacIntyre is surely correct, and you can see why if you consider some non-living object. Take a familiar object, the moon. How should we describe the structure of the moon? First, we would describe the shape of the moon (spherical) and the location of the moon (in orbit around Earth, which in turn orbits the sun). We might move on to list prominent features of the moon's surface ("seas," craters, etc.) and the moon's interior. Notice that this description is mostly static; the history of the moon would only come into play in order to explain how some current feature of the moon came to be. With human beings, matters are reversed. It is possible to talk about the current state of a person—right

---

2. MacIntyre, *After Virtue*. See pp. 208ff.

now, he weighs a certain amount, he is lying in bed, he is dreaming, his pulse rate is so many beats per minute, and so on. But if we were limited to a description of the current state of a person, we would miss most of what we consider important about him. Human beings, like all living things, change over the course of their lives; they are first and foremost *historical* beings. The only way to make sense of a human life is to relate the different times of a person's life to each other.

Personalize that last sentence. The only way to make sense of my life is to relate the different times of my life to each other.

How do we do this? *We remember.* True, we remember only a tiny portion of our experiences, feelings, thoughts, and emotions. (Can you remember anything about the twelfth day after your twelfth birthday?) The things we do remember become important to us because we weave them into the story we tell ourselves about ourselves.

Suppose you meet someone new. You want to "get to know" this new acquaintance. What do you ask? You ask for parts of her story— the people she has known (perhaps you know them too), where she has been, what she has done, etc. To be sure, you also want to know aspects of her current state—what does she think about the new movie? Does she like lattés? And so on. But you would never think that you really knew a person if you only knew her current state.

The movie *Memento* (2000) eerily underscores the importance of memory. In this story (notice: narrative again) a man suffers a brain injury that prevents him from transferring short-term memory into long-term memory. Every time he wakes up, he has forgotten everything that happened to him since the injury. While he is awake, he is fully aware of his current state and the events of that particular day. But since he cannot form new long-term memories, his life disintegrates disastrously.

To be an integrated self, one must be able to describe one's own life as a sensible story. Often we tell bits of our story to others, but the most important audience for personal narrative is the self. Since I am a historical being, the only way to make sense of who I am now is to relate my current state to my past.

When we speak of a person's life "making sense," we do not imply that all events in that person's life are all of a piece. The narrative of a person's life may include drastic changes of direction: "That was my life up until the accident . . . " or, "Everything kept getting worse and worse, but then I started going to AA . . . " Notice that by such moves we explain how a person's life is a single life, even though it has undergone radical change. An illness, a new job, a college degree, a change of location, a death of someone else, and so on—there are many factors that may explain significant change in a person's life.

What would we say about a life that exhibited radical changes, but without any such explanation? Suppose on one day "Eve" is a kind, generous neighbor while the next day she is cruel and suspicious, and the day after that she is a motorcycle moll? There are such people; some have been diagnosed as having associative identity disorder. (It used to be called "multiple personality disorder.") Notice that this diagnosis allows other people, relatives and psychological professionals who deal with the patient, to make *some* kind of sense of the person's life; they do so by attributing the patient's bizarre changes to disease. But what about Eve, herself? Unless she makes therapeutic progress, her life is thoroughly disintegrated. She doesn't know who she is.

People who suffer personality disorders are extreme cases. Everyday, garden-variety disintegration doesn't put people in the hospital. At least, not usually—who knows how many people suffer serious depression because they cannot make sense of the various roles they play?

When a person's life has no meaningful connecting narrative, he may feel that life is just "one damn thing after another." He does things, and other people do things that impinge on his life, but it is as if the events in his life are simply tokens collected on a string. Each token-event is completely loose and separate; nothing connects the times of his life into a life. Nothing gives significance to the whole.

The key to integration, then, is to construct a narrative of one's life that makes sense of the events in one's life. The things I do today, the people I care about now, the hopes I have for the future—all these parts of my life grow out of my past and my beliefs and values. My life makes sense to me.

It is not enough to have a story of one's private life. Alasdair MacIntyre points out that the stories we tell ourselves always relate our individual histories to some larger story. For millions of people in the twentieth century, the larger story was Marx's story of the coming revolution; they were able to find significance in their own struggles because they saw them as part of something great and good. Other political ideologies offer a similar benefit: by working to elect so-and-so or to change some social policy, you can understand yourself as contributing to the common good, a better life for many people.

The larger story may have to do with group identity. The individual sees her life as part of the history of "our people." Imagine a Jewish family living in America. In many ways they are assimilated into popular American culture—they go to movies, love baseball, and frequent the public library. But they also make an effort to maintain certain Jewish traditions, such as attending worship or observing Jewish holidays. They incorporate these practices into their personal stories, into their identity. The larger story of "our people" gives background and significance to the traditions.

Other families may not hold to religious beliefs, but they may honor family traditions. Again, this is a way for the individual to place the story of his life in a larger context. "My family" replaces "our people." Large stories may be ideological, religious, cultural, or some combination of factors.

We have mentioned several larger stories, often called "meta-narratives" by postmodernist philosophers. We've made reference to Platonism, Hegelianism, Marxism, Judaism, family traditions, etc. Some thinkers have said that the lack of a meta-narrative is the crucial fact of postmodern times. The postmodern philosopher, Jean-François Lyotard, wrote, "I define postmodern as incredulity toward meta-narratives."[3] To the degree that Lyotard's attitude is shared by other postmodernists, they thereby create a barrier to personal integration. Integration is only possible by means of narrative, and because human beings are social creatures, they inevitably want a personal story that connects them to the larger world. If Lyotard is right—if the postmodern person simply discounts all meta-narratives because she finds them incredible—then it is no surprise that more and more people today suffer disintegrated lives.

THE STORY OF THE BIBLE

In the history of western civilization, one narrative dwarfs all others in terms of its social importance. Judaism, Christianity and Islam are all rooted in the story of the Bible. For centuries the Bible has supplied the meta-narrative for people groups in Asia, Africa, Europe and the Americas. More than half the people in the world today are adherents of these religions. To one degree or another, the story of the Bible provides an integrating structure for these people's lives.

3. Lyotard, *The Postmodern Condition.* See his introduction. Also available in Perry Anderson (1998). *The Origins of Postmodernity.* London/New York: Verso, pp. 24–27.

(Notice that we say "to one degree or another." In point of fact, we think the disintegrating pressures of advertising and entertainment quite overwhelm the biblical narrative for millions of nominal Jews, Christians, and Muslims.)

What is the story of the Bible? In outline, it's not very complicated. (1) God created the universe, including human beings. (2) Since God is good, the world God created is good, and God intends that human beings flourish. (3) Something went wrong in God's creation; i.e. evil/sin became part of human life in the world. Consequently, human life often falls far short of flourishing. (4) God remains good and will not abandon creation; instead, God acts in history to redeem/save/rescue human beings. (5) In the end, God will complete the process of redemption, and human beings will experience the kind of life God wants for them.

That's the outline. In detail, and there is much detail in the Bible, things are more complicated. For instance, Jews, Christians, and Muslims disagree fundamentally about *how* God redeems/rescues human beings. (Does God redeem by making a covenant with Israel, by sending Jesus the Messiah, or by commissioning the Prophet to proclaim submission to God?) Within each religion, believers disagree about many points of doctrine, so that there are distinct branches of Judaism, Christianity, and Islam.

In chapter 6, we gave reasons why we believe Christianity is true. We think God acted to save humanity by living among us as Jesus the Messiah. But we do not deny that God made a covenant with Israel, nor do we deny that God spoke to the Prophet.[4] Judaism, Christianity, and Islam all have conceptual resources to enable people to integrate their lives. According to the Bible's narrative, human beings were designed by God to flourish when they are rightly related to God. The Bible identifies God as the Creator, Redeemer, and Lover of humanity.[5] If we give attention to these characteristics of the God of the Bible, we can discover how to integrate our lives.

---

4. We do deny that the covenant with Israel is *complete* without Messiah Jesus, and we deny that the revelation made to Muhammad *supercedes* the revelation of God in Jesus, the Son of God.

5. Some believers would add that the Bible presents God in other roles; in particular, God is the eternal Judge of all human beings. This is a crucial aspect of God, they would argue, because it enshrines justice as a basic human value. We certainly agree that God is just, but God's justice expresses itself in redemption.

GOD'S NATURE AND OUR VOCATION

According to the creation story in Genesis, God made the human race "in God's image." (And the text specifically says God made humanity "male and female." We wish that Western history had been shaped more by that thought than Aristotle's speculations about the nature of the sexes!)

Many theologians—Jewish, Christian, and Muslim—have interpreted the notion of the *Imago Dei* (the image of God) in terms borrowed from Greek philosophers. We are like God, theologians said, in that we are spiritual and rational beings. God transcends the physical world; surely it is not by virtue of our bodies that we are like God, as if God had physical parts! So the reasoning went. If you follow this line of thought further, as many theologians did, you can end up devaluing bodily life altogether. You can begin to think we honor God best when we restrain and deny our physical desires. Spirituality gets associated with asceticism. You begin to believe we can never be at home in the world, since we really belong in heaven.

Rather than conceiving God as a rational being first and foremost, we will do better to meditate on God's roles in the biblical narrative. God is the Creator, the Redeemer, and the Lover. In each case, human beings are called to be like God.

Dorothy Sayers and other recent thinkers point out that Genesis 1:26–27, which introduces the idea of *Imago Dei*, occurs as part of the story of *creation*. God is the creator beyond all others, but we also create. When we express our creative nature, we are like God. J.R.R. Tolkien suggested the term "sub-creator" for the kind of work artists and poets do. They take the raw materials of this world (stone, paint, language) to make something new.

Does God call every person to be a sub-creator? Maybe! Creativity is not limited to artists, musicians, and writers. Take a clue from the Greek root of "poem," *poiema*, a creation or making. When human beings make things, they become sub-creators. The thing made may be a loaf of bread, a flower or vegetable garden, a story, a business plan, a picture, a farm, a bridge, a haircut, and so on. (One might even express creativity by writing a philosophy book!)

We believe God intends that human beings create. In a sense, God's initial act of creation is incomplete, and it falls to us to fill in the gaps. To put it another way: God continues to create the world, in that he calls us to be sub-creators. When we act as sub-creators, we take our intended place in the world; we are at home in the world.

Not all our "makings" are of equal value. Sometimes we hurry and fail to do good work. We get lazy and sloppy. Sometimes we even forget that beauty is possible. So some of our "makings" turn out ugly, cheap, cruel, or useless. We must not be satisfied with this; we should strive for excellence in our making.

Not all of us "makers" are of equal ability. There are better bakers, better painters, better builders, better organizers, better hair stylists, and better writers than we are. Such differences should not bother us. We are not called to make as well as Tolstoy or Tolkien; we are called to make as well as we can.[6]

The human ability to create is linked with our delight in play. Just as it is natural for people to make things, it is natural for them to play. We display and show off our makings. We laugh, we dance, we sign our books, we display our paintings, and we sit down to a meal—over and over in diverse ways we take joy in our makings. Sometimes making something is such hard work that we may forget to rejoice and play. At such times, it helps to glance back over one's work, like the farmer at the end of a long day: "Who woulda believed it? I can plow a *pretty* field."

"Vocation" is an English word based on the Latin word, *vocare*, to call. In contemporary speech, people often use "vocation" to mean "career." We mean something more than that. A vocation is a calling. As we understand the Bible's narrative, God the Creator *calls* us to be creators too. As our examples have emphasized, there are many kinds of sub-creation. My creative calling will be different from yours.

Here is the first way to build integration into your life. We invite you to see yourself as called by God to be a maker. Be at home in the world; be a sub-creator.

The story of creation is found mostly in the first two chapters of Genesis. By contrast, the story of redemption is strewn throughout the Bible. God acted at various times and in diverse ways to turn humanity back to a right relationship with God. God made a covenant with Abraham and his descendants, the people of Israel, promising to be their God and through them bless the world. God communicated to Israel through the law (Torah) and the preaching of the prophets, always with the aim of using Israel to bring all the people of the world back to God.

---

6. Tolkien displayed this truth in the delightful story, "Leaf by Niggle." Niggle, a painter, longed to paint glorious landscapes, but he was actually competent at painting leaves. In the fullness of time, a "leaf by Niggle" became a thing of eternal beauty. Tolkien, "Leaf by Niggle," 100–120.

As Christians, we believe God's crowning act of redemption came in the life, death, and resurrection of Jesus.

What does this mean for our vocation? God is the redeemer. As Jesus said, God is like a housewife who searches diligently for a lost coin; God is like a father who longs for his lost son to come home. God wants to bring humanity back into a healthy relationship with himself.

The first century Christian apostle Paul wrote specifically about himself and other Christian preachers when he wrote in 2 Corinthians, "We are therefore Christ's ambassadors, as though God were making his appeal through us. We implore you on Christ's behalf: Be reconciled to God." What Paul says about himself is true of believers in general. God *calls* us to be ministers of reconciliation.

Are we all to be Christian preachers? Well, in one sense, yes! Remember that often the loudest speech is one without words. Christians are called to *live out* reconciliation—reconciliation between God and human persons, reconciliation between the human race and its natural environment, and reconciliation between people.

Here is another way to think about it. Christians often repeat the words of the prayer Jesus taught his disciples: "Your kingdom come, your will be done on earth as it is in heaven." The ministry of reconciliation happens whenever Christians put feet to this prayer. There are many different ways Christians can respond to God's call to serve the kingdom of God.

We can give to meet human needs. We can comfort people who suffer. We can campaign for public policies we think will protect peace and benefit the commonwealth. We can teach. We can recognize and praise the good. We can stand against prejudice, ugliness, and immorality. We can invite people to believe in Christ. When we do such things, we participate in God's redemption of the world.

Any time people strive to do God's will on earth, they are responding to God's call. So here is the second way to build integration into your life. We invite you to see yourself as called by God to the ministry of reconciliation. Be at home in the world; be a reconciler and redeemer.

So far we have mentioned creation and redemption. God's creative and redeeming work flow out of God's deepest characteristic. Before all time, at the end of time, underlying all God is and does—God is love. We want to emphasize this point, taking our cues from the medieval Christian mystic, Julian of Norwich.

God does not love you a little; God is passionately concerned that you find perfect happiness. God does not love you from a distance; God is closer to you than your clothes. God does not love you abstractly; in Jesus, God suffered as you suffer. God does not merely wish for your good; God is doing all that can be done to bring you to full maturity as a child of God. God always has loved you and will love you forever. God's love for you is more real than any thought or feeling you have ever had. God's love will triumph in the end.

God is the Lover *par excellence*. But we can be like God; we can be little lovers. This is the third part of our vocation. God *calls* us to love.

There are different kinds of love, and the Greek language gives us names for some of them. First, there is family love, *storge*, the love of parents for children and nephews for aunts. Second, there is *philia*, the love shared by friends. (Some philosophers, such as Aristotle, considered *philia* especially important. Friendship, Aristotle said, was one of the chief reasons people live in cities.) Third, there is *eros*, romantic love, with all of its power for good and ill. But the most basic kind of love, the bedrock love that supports all the others, is *agape*. According to the New Testament, *agape* is the best word for God's love.

Agape is love that pays attention. Human beings struggle with selfishness—not just the selfishness that tries to grab and take, but the kind of selfishness that sees other people as things. Whenever we see another person as something useful, something attractive, something repulsive, something scary, or *any* kind of "thing," we aren't really paying attention. To really see another person, we have to let our own concerns fade into the background. People are not things, and the heart of love is to see them as they really are. Learning to pay attention is a lifelong project. Though it is not easy, we believe people can get better at it.

This, then, is the third way to build integration into your life. We invite you to see yourself as called by God to be a lover. Be at home in the world; be a lover.

The vocations we have described are general vocations. We think they apply to all of us. They are not mutually exclusive. You can express creativity, work for reconciliation, and love people at the same time.

In the course of a person's life, she or he will discover or invent specific ways of implementing the general vocations. One person will be a teacher, another a farmer, another an inventor, and so on. Whatever the particulars of your life story, we invite you to see them as the living out of creativity, reconciliation, and love. We invite you to see your life as part of the grand story of Jesus, the Messiah.

Addendum

Christian Apologetics Resources

A S WE SAY IN chapter 1, our approach to apologetics differs significantly from many other writers' work. We have not tried to produce conclusive arguments. We don't want to coerce readers into faith, even if it were possible. We hope, instead, to have offered an invitation into faith.

Nevertheless, we still have great respect for the work of other Christian apologists. We've learned much from them, and we've borrowed some of their ideas in this book. We strongly encourage readers who have interest in apologetics to pursue that leaning. With very little effort, you can find dozens of books on apologetics, and in a short time online you will discover many websites devoted to arguing for or against religious belief. As with most human activities, the quality of work ranges from very good to very bad, so read critically. In this addendum, we make no attempt to be thorough; we are merely providing a list of some good resources.

Alston, Wm. P. *Perceiving God: The Epistemology of Religious Experience*. Ithaca: Cornell University Press, 1991.

Capon, Robert Farrar. *The Third Peacock: A Book About God and the Problem of Evil*. New York: Image, 1972.

Chesterton, G.K. *Orthodoxy*. New York: Image, 1959.

Clark, Kelly James. *When Faith is Not Enough*. Grand Rapids: Eerdmans, 1997.

———, ed. *Philosophers Who Believe: The Spiritual Journeys of 11 Leading Thinkers*. Downers Grove: InterVarsity, 1993.

Edgar, William and K. Scoot Oliphint. *Christian Apologetics: Past and Present*. Vol. 1: To 1500. Wheaton: Crossway, 2009.

Habermas, Gary and Michael Licona. *The Case for the Resurrection of Jesus*. Kregel, 2004.

Lewis, C .S. *Mere Christianity*. New York: MacMillan, 1943.

———. *The Weight of Glory and Other Addresses*. New York: Collier, 1975.

Markos, Louis. *Apologetics for the 21st Century*. Wheaton: Crossway, 2010.

McLeod-Harrison, Mark S. *Repairing Eden: Humility, Mysticism and the Existential Problem of Religious Diversity*. Montreal: McGill-Queens University Press, 2005.

———. *Rationality and Theistic Belief: An Essay on Reformed Epistemology*. Ithaca: Cornell University Press, 1993.

Morris, Thomas. *God and the Philosophers: The Reconciliation of Faith and Reason*. Oxford: Oxford University Press, 1996.

Murray, Michael, ed. *Reason for the Hope Within*. Grand Rapids: Eerdmans, 1999. (Apologists will find a great variety of topics addressed here, by sixteen good philosophers. Of particular interest might be Robin Collins' essay, "A Scientific Argument for the Existence of God: The Fine-Tuning Design Argument.")

Nicholi, Armand. *The Question of God: C.S. Lewis and Sigmund Freud Debate God, Love, Sex, and the Meaning of Life*. New York: Simon and Schuster, 2002.

Overman, Dean. *A Case for the Existence of God*. Lanham: Rowman & Littlefield, 2009.

Plantinga, Alvin. *God and Other Minds*. Ithaca: Cornell University Press, 1967. Paperback edition, 1990.

———. *Warrant and Proper Function*. Oxford: Oxford University Press, 1993. (In particular, chapter 12: "Is Naturalism Irrational?" will be of interest to apologists.)

———. *The Analytic Theist*. Grand Rapids: Eerdmans, 1998. (This collection of essays has several of interest to apologists, including "The Freewill Defense," "Reason and Belief in God," and "The Ontological Argument.")

Wennberg, Robert N. *Faith at the Edge: A Book for Doubters*. Grand Rapids: Eerdmans, 2009.

Wolterstorff, Nicholas. *Reason within the Bounds of Religion*. 2nd ed. Grand Rapids: Eerdmans, 1984.

Bibliography

Habermas, Gary. *The Resurrection of Jesus: An Apologetic*. Grand Rapids: Baker, 1980.

Habermas, Gary, and Michael Licona. *The Case for the Resurrection of Jesus*. Grand Rapids: Kregel, 2004.

Hick, John. *An Interpretation of Religion*. 2nd ed. New Haven: Yale University Press, 2005.

Lewis, C.S. *The Last Battle*. San Francisco: HarperCollins, 1994.

Lyotard, Jean-Francois. *The Postmodern Condition*. Minneapolis: University of Minnesota Press, 1984.

MacIntyre, Alasdair. *After Virtue*. Notre Dame: University of Notre Dame Press, 1981.

Martel, Yann. *The Life of Pi*. Orlando: Harcourt Books, 2001.

Pelikan, Jaroslav. *Jesus through the Centuries*. New Haven: Yale University Press, 1985.

Russell, Bertrand. *Why I am not a Christian and Other Essays on Religion and Related Subjects*. New York: Allen and Unwin, 1957.

Tolkien, J.R.R. "Leaf by Niggle," *The Tolkien Reader*. New York: Ballantine Books, 1966.

Whitehead, Alfred North, and Bertrand Russell. *Principia Mathematica*. 3 vols. Cambridge: Cambridge University Press, 1910–1913. Second edition, 1925 (Vol. 1), 1927 (Vols. 2, 3).

Williams, Margery. *The Velveteen Rabbit: Or How Toys Become Real*. New York: Doubleday, 1922.

Wittgenstein, Ludwig. *Tractatus Logico-Philosophicus*. London: Routledge & Kegan Paul, 1961. First German edition, 1921.

Subject/Name Index

Alston, William, 110
apologetics, ix, 1–4, 13, 16, 26, 77, 131
Aquinas, Thomas, 19, 24, 51
Aristotle, 19, 22–24, 51, 105, 127, 130
Augustine, 20, 24

Berkeley, George, 27, 28, 32
big bang cosmology, 52–53, 55–56
Buddhism, 68, 72, 76, 81, 83–87

Camus, Albert, 34–36
cause & effect, 29, 31, 33, 34
causes & reasons, 99–100
Christianity, 2, 11–13, 16, 24, 62, 68–72,
    74–77, 78, 80, 83, 86–87, 90,
    92, 94, 96–98, 101, 105–107,
    109–111, 116, 125–126
community(ies), 10, 14, 15, 16, 79
"completed science," 43, 47, 49
Confucianism, 90–92

Descartes, Rene, 4, 7, 20, 25–27, 36
determinism, 44, 45, 46, 48
"disintegration," 3, 21, 37–39, 117–118,
    120, 122–126
doubt, 8, 10, 11, 15, 39–40

Einstein, Albert, 50
Enlightenment, 34
epistemology, 25, 27, 30–34
essence(s), 22, 30, 34–36, 87
evolution, 43–44, 45–46, 55, 59–60
exclusivism, 62, 65–66, 69–72
existentialism, 34–36, 120–121
extraterrestrials, 42

"fine tuning," 53–55
"flourishing," 15, 18–20, 23–24, 34, 39,
    68, 74, 92, 105, 107, 114, 116,
    117, 126
Fordmakers, 81–82
free will, 33, 35, 44, 48, 49, 50, 79, 86,
    112, 120, 132
Freud, Sigmund, 104
Freudian suspicion, 6–8, 51, 104

Gautama, Siddhartha, 83–86, 89
Gödel, Kurt, 58
God of the gaps, 45–46, 48–50
God's call (vocation), 15, 117, 119, 121,
    12, 125, 127–130
good arguments, 2–3

Habermas, Gary, 101–102
Heisenberg, Werner, 50
hierarchy of sciences, 44–45
Hilbert, David, 58
Hinduism, 68–72, 74–76, 81, 87–90
holiness movement, 5
hope, 8, 40, 47, 92, 108–110, 114–115,
    124, 132
Hubble, Edwin, 52
Hume, David, 27, 28–33, 36, 38, 84, 110,
    120

image of God, 24, 127
inclusivism, 62, 66–67, 73–76, 78, 80, 98
insulin, 17–18, 37
"integration," 4, 15–16, 19, 20, 39, 117–
    119, 121–122, 124–130
intellectual property, 17, 37
invitation, 1, 2, 15, 63
Islam, 68, 71–72, 76, 95–96

Jainism, 68, 81–83
Jesus, 9–15, 24, 68, 71, 74–76, 78–80,
        95–96, 98, 100–107, 110–112,
        114–116, 126, 129–131
Judaism, 68–69, 72, 76, 92–95
Julian of Norwich, 103, 129–130

Kant, Immanuel, 4, 30–36, 38, 48, 110
karma, 82, 84, 88–90
Kierkegaard, Soren, 35
K'ung (Confucius), 90–92

Leibniz, Gottfried, 27, 57
Lewis, C.S., 2, 73, 133
li, 90–91
Life of Pi, 62, 67–68
Locke, John 27–28, 31, 36
love, 15, 43, 46–48, 62, 74, 87, 92, 104,
        107–108, 111–112, 114–116,
        126–127, 129–130
Lyotard, J–F., 125

MacIntyre, Alasdair, 122, 124
Marcel, Gabriel, 8, 35, 109
Marx, Karl 7, 8, 51, 119, 124
Martel, Yann, 62, 133
Memento, 123
messiah, 94–95, 126, 130
metaphysics, 25
modernism, 8, 11, 16, 20, 21, 25–27, 34,
        38–40, 41–61, 119
Mohammed, 95–96
multi–universe model, 56
mystery, 8, 15, 40, 41, 46–61, 62–63, 67,
        69, 78–79, 83, 86, 90, 97, 109,
        115, 120
Myth of Sisyphus 34–35

naturalism, 16, 28–29, 38, 40, 41–61,
        62–63, 67, 78, 80, 104–105, 119,
        120, 132
Newton, Isaac, 50, 57
Nietzsche, Friedrich. 7, 8
Nirvana, 68, 72, 84–87
noumenal world, 33

oscillating universe, 54–56

pacifism, 82–83, 86
phenomenal world, 33
Plantinga, Alvin, 60, 110, 112, 132
Plato, 2, 4, 20, 22
Planck time, 52, 54
pluralism, 62, 64–65, 68–69, 72–73
porcine philosophy, 17, 37
postmodernism, 7–8, 16, 17, 21, 27,
        36–40, 69, 80, 120–122, 125–126,
        133
"pure thinker," 4, 20–21, 23, 25, 30, 34,
        108
quantum dynamics, 50–51, 53, 79

rebirth/reincarnation, 72, 81, 82, 84,
        87–88
Russell, Bertrand, 52, 57–58
Rousseau, J–J., 4
reductionism, 45, 46
resurrection, 74, 76, 80, 94–95, 98, 100–
        104, 110–111, 129, 131, 133

Sayers, Dorothy, 127
Schrödinger, Erwin, 50
Seinfeld, 120
skepticism, 26, 28–30
Socrates, 2, 4, 20, 117
Spinoza, 27
suffering, 112–114

theory choice, 43
Tillich, Paul, 35
Tolkien, J.R.R., 127–128
Tolstoy, Leo, 128
Trinity, 96, 111, 114

Vedic religion, 81, 87
Velveteen rabbit, 116

Whitehead, Alfred, 57–58
wisdom, 10, 13, 19, 20
worldview, 1, 8, 16, 38, 41–42, 80

Scripture Index

Genesis

1:26-27   127

Acts

2:31   100
3:15   100
4:12   75
10:40   100
11:22–25   102
13:37   100

1 Corinthians

15:1–5   101
15:14   100

2 Corinthians

5:20   129

Galatians

1:17   102
3:6–18   75

CPSIA information can be obtained
at www.ICGtesting.com
Printed in the USA
BVHW041149051121
620883BV00011B/223

9 781610 970716